my HEART speaks

TANYA TURTON

Copyright © 2020 Tanya Turton

Copyright remains the property of the author and apart from any fair dealing for the purposes of private study, research, criticism or review, as permitted under the Copyright Act, no part may be reproduced by any process without written permission. All inquiries should be made to the author.

Typeset & Cover by Chain of Hearts Creative

National Library of Australia - ISBN-978-0-6488739-3-8

MY HEART SPEAKS

Flow free these words of love for you to hear into, for they are so intently spoken with you in mind it is to see. You are of the one true love that is to be mine and in this I see of the all that you are to be in me. In this love that I sit to feel as mine, I do not dwell on what it is not, but only of all that it be. For you are to be my true loves in all that you are to speak as mine to hear. And in this I feel of the greatest intent within to know of you as true and loyal in your words to speak and in this I offer to you my heart wide opened and willing in trust to receive. It is in welcoming & receiving of this love that I be for I know of this love; I remember it well for this love is me as I sit in here to see. No truer words are to be spoken in my willingness to ask of this love that you are to be mine in all of eternity to be of this that it is....

YOU, ME, I, AND THE ALL THAT BE.

CHAPTER ONE

HEART SPEAKS

In one's heart to be heard is the all that we are to comprehend as the very being of the truest essence of self to be realised into. Is it not to be spoken of here for all that are to ask or listen into, that this beating heart of yours is the true feeler, the true communicator of this that is seen as you, is beating in time within this very essence of us to be seen as.

For all hearts are to beat as one, are they not. It is the god speak within that we are all to hear of the greater creator of this that we be to speak. In this inner knowing, this voice that speaks of great wisdom, in here one is to feel with certainty as though it is to be their own. One must, for it is in these words to comprehend to know of that they are yours in your truth to hear as this that we are of you all to be. One's heart is the true communicator and it is of this that we have spoken into this to say many times.

In this heart that is in wanting to speak her true voice that one will recognise as their own to speak, is where the findings of self to be realised into are. In this heart that is to be ever so slightly opened within each space of recognition, into this you are to hear of that you will feel this gentle tugging from within to allow for the heart to be ever present in this spoken offering of self to be. When one is to sit into oneself and ask for this heart of theirs to speak these words of encouragement and love it is that you as the receiver of these words to be heard will find the internal growth to flow filling and completing self to be asking of more in a recognition of this to be. In the previewing of self in the eyes of the heart, {in this we are to mean the intense unveiling of these hidden hurts and emotions of unsaid words to express}, is where the words of endearment are to be recognised as yours to speak of with such intention as to this that you are asking of self to become. We speak not of the conversations that one is to have within this thinking mind to be, it is the words of heart felt that one is to really listen to in the exact moment of which it feels the need to arise from within. One's gracious heart is to elevate the intense feelings of the hardened heart that sits into this human form as the recogniser of all that they are to hear, see and say, for it is not of this heavy heart that one must feel attached to.

Our hearts are in this place of trueness to be spoken of and in this space that one is to call their own true heart connection it is that one will feel all that we speak of as to be ours in the understanding of self to be this that hears. It is of only this space into this that we are to connect and to think of it as to be any other way is incorrect for all limitations that one is to put upon oneself in the asking of this to be felt as heart speak will feel the nonsense talk and the intrusion of self to be thought of as an inability to see perfection within.

This heart space that is bold in this speaking is of yours to hear and one must never enter into these external conversations of not to be and it is often in discussion with self and others that are not of this place to sit into that will allow the indecisions of this to be heard as your wrong truths.

This heart space that you speak of is mine, is it not?

It is of this space that ones such as yourselves are to call heart space but the real intention of this space to be within you to feel is to be the ever constant reminder of this that you are to be magnificent, truly magical and ever evolving and eternal of this lovingness that you are to become of. We see this space spoken of as something that one is to obtain in many offerings from others to speak of it as such to be. Allowance within must be given to all that are in this position of which it is to ask, that you will in definiteness see to feel of this opening within your form to be of a wanting to be in this space to receive. IN the listening that one undertakes, is in all its correctness offered to you to hear, in this very moment one is to hear these words to feel good within, know that one will recognise the greatest of intentions that these words spoken are for you to hear. We sit in recognition of this space to be asked from within you to feel into once more for the heart is to travel with you into the all that you become of. We offer to you to hear into it is not of the physical heart to be everlasting but of the eternal heart that is to be the innerness that is yours to reside into as the one truth of this that we are within you.

MANY speak of thy heart as the god space within, why is this so?

When one is to refer to this as the god space within, is it not to label this as a sensing of importance or to speak of this as an aspect of yourself to be thought of as another? For all that is contained into these thoughts of this to be of the god that lays within is to be thinking that he is to be the offeror of these words to hear into, this we offer it is not.

You are to be the voice of reason and strong belief into which it is that one is to sit. You are the knower of this self to be if you are in agreeance with the all that is to flow forth from within you in this space that we speak of as your eternal heart that speaks so wanting to

YOU.

I hear this voice speaking but is it mine?

In the asking of this voice of yours to be heard, one must be of a willingness to hear into correction without conviction of self in the need to explain of all that they are to do as in a negative approval of this self to be heard or described. In ones such as you this we are to see, to offer that the many of you that are ever so willing to ask others to be your responder in this that you think it is that you need them to answer you in questioning of self to be. You will hear not of your own truth but entirely of theirs being voiced. It is said here that in their offering is to be only a reflection from within themselves as the how and why it is for them that they are to see this that you are.

Be in a willingness to hear of all the kind that is to be passed through you to this that you be for it is in their simple yet easy way of which it is that one is to feel this transitioning of self to go through to become the ever true receiver of this that is yours to hear into. It is of you to become whole and complete within one's thoughts to think of self to be again. For we see of you as the holder of this that is to be so great and even truly magical, to be said in the truth of which it is to be recognised and in this seeing of the all that you are the holder of within in this you will envision the beautiful you that you are that is to sit intently within me.

In spirits heart I speak to capture the true understanding of how and of what should be felt, do I not?

If one is to feel as though it is of us that is to offer to speak, then it shall in your entirety of truth be yours to hear into.

We seek not of the all to be heard in this way, as such to repeat to others of what it is that we speak. All intention is to come from within this that you be and it is of this great intention within that is asking of you to hear into this space of which it is to receive, to hear of us speak in truth of this that shall be offered.

Thankyou.

OUR TURN TO SPEAK

We are intentional beings of grace, love, and compassion. It is of us to soar beyond any beliefs or thoughts of us to be that you in this form as human have of us to be. We are intentional in the offering of love to be received from you with this gracious heart of hearts to be yours to feel of us to be yours. IN this it is that we offer this to be felt by you in your truth of this to be heard into for it is only of your willingness to be allowing of this heart to be willing to be felt within that you will feel this guidance to become of yours to remember as this to be you. In all shapes and forms that we are to present to ones such as yourselves to connect into it is only of this true identity to be known as this energy of the times that be in this current now of yours to sit into that it is to be felt as a strong urging from within your heart to feel of us to know in such a sacred truth to become that it is of us that speak.

In the thinking of us to be a sort after prize or an addition to your resume it is to be offered here to you to hear into that it cannot nor will it ever be received in this fashion of which it is to speak. It is in the rawness of honesty that it is to be felt with such the greatest of intentions to feel into and to speak this of us to be will find its way into your hearts opening to be felt in all its realness that it is to speak of here to hear into. We are in genuine space of this reality it appears for you to realise into and one must adjust the internal thinking or the minds thoughts of such that we are not obtainable to the average jo. So to offer here often it is just this to speak that the unobtrusive questioner to be willing to just accept of us as we are to be with no thoughts attached to of what or who it is that we are, are to be the true receivers of this that we speak of.

In ones heart to be seen by us in the plenty there are many situations that are stirred from within to the external becoming of such that one is to find themselves drawn into to think of this that be us is to be in the offering to one is the last resort. This is Yes, often in cases to be presented to be seen by many that in the down and out of life one is to release all expectations and totally give in to these feelings of overwhelment to receive of this that is to open the heart to this offering to be felt as real. But let us offer to you to hear into that in ones that are to ask it is not of us to require or ask any of you to be in this such described position of life to be able to interact to the degree of seeing to hear, to feel of us to be. For it is our knowing of all that are to be present in this life form and the many that are existence in this reality and space of pure adrenalin to become, to know that they are to be the ever eternal carriers of this phenomenal love to be felt as theirs and theirs alone, always united in formation of the exactness that this one the true creator is to be yours within. In this being of love an light that we are spoken of often in thoughts of us to present as an understanding of such that we are to be visioned as, we feel the intent that is put to these thoughts of us to be ever presented to you in this way and it is of ones understanding of thought to be that we are. We are the travellers of all eternity it is to appear and if it is to be spoken of it is this that we are to be ever residing into without the need to become of this that you see us to be. For we are ever in the essence of true plausibility it would be correct to offer suggesting to ones such as yourselves to ask that we are ever present in this that we be.

Of us it is to offer that you are continually surrounded by this that we choose of ourselves to be seen into. It is to speak of this that we do not offer any suggestions as such for we are many and yet one in all that we be to stand, to suggest, to speak and it is in this that one must release any conceptional ideas as to the how's and whys of this dimension that we are to sit within.

We fear not of ones misplacing in thoughts of this to be and the wandering mind that is searching as we speak to offer a thought of coherent understanding to this description that we offer is to be a confusing one to look at from the human place in which it is that one is present.   We seek not of one to delve to deeply within to grasp of this that we speak for you are all of this that we be just into another offering of such that you so chose to undertake to participate into.

> *We are the entirety of which it is that you are to represent to self to see. It is in this external way in which it is to view of self to be wayward in your thoughts of all that you are to present to the ever-seeing eyes of human position to be. This you are not, and it is in this we wish to speak to know of, that you are the grace of the ALL that be and it is in this way that we wish the most to always see of you be.*

Let us speak of the Love and Heart felt space complete within us ALL.

When one's heart is full of love,

It is in this we wish to distinguish the difference that is to be felt as the human form of love that the many of you are to possess or to be ever in the external searching of this love as described to be felt. For often it is felt to be received by that of another that is to return this love in respect of you to be or it is to search ever always to the asking of others to represent this love or offer it to you to be of.

It is in this that we see the human component of self to think of themselves in this way regarding the topic of love to be.

You are to ask of another to provide you with this companionship/love, is this not correct?

You are to require another to provide a dedication to you in this love to feel, are you not?

You are to respect of those that love you in all that they offer, is this not correct?

One can only see of their worthiness if it is to please this of another to let them think into this way, Is this not correct?

You are to think that the love of or from another is to be ever bolder than yours, are you not?

The list is endless regarding the opportunities or situations that this life in your participation to be was your choosing of love to be so.

In this re-entering many of you have forgotten this great love in earnest to be yours so deeply embedded within you patiently waiting to be discovered once again as your ever provider of this to be yours to know instantly and eternally that this *LOVE* is you.

There are many that claim to be the willing participants into these offerings from another as to be the life that they live their lives into and it is of this great love that they are to feel complete, Is this not to speak of?

In this we ask of those that see this to be the way to sense deep within themselves to discover of the trueness that sits within them to ask of these words. Is it the love of yourself that allows you to shine so decisively bright that not of another could ever match these rays of yours to beam? Or is it that ones such as yourself are intuitively in tuned within this loving being that you are and in this so doing to know of that you are complete first in your own true love, your own grand love, your own big love, to offer here to be heard that it does not or would not matter if this one was to express this to be not of theirs to offer to you.

When one is to see only of their own BIG LOVE first then you are in the complete knowing of true love to be yours.

CHAPTER TWO

MIRACLES OF LOVE

IN these words offered here to speak into it is to relay that in a miracle ones such as yourselves are to only expect this as expectations to be sought whether in distress, illness or to be so far reaching to be that one is to see of not many. It is offered here to say that in this we have spoken to many in this way that the receiving of a miracle is to be offered here to say that you are the true miracle of this that be and are this place in which it is that one in this form and all forms to be recognised offer this that you and all are the true miracle of self to become into.

YOU as 'I' ARE THE MIRACLE THAT WE SPEAK OF TO SEE.

I am taking off my blinkers,

Are you willing to take off your blinkers of non-coherency to believe in this as a major feat of the heavens to shift and the gods above to perform these miraculous feats of which it is to think that one must be deserving of to receive.

It is in this offering of truth to say that your miracles are YOU. In every way to be seen into and it is to feel the removal of all thoughts attached in this way of what it is to think of a miracle to stand out to you to be, for it is in this that we offer, get ready to see this in a new way.

"Miracles are to be your everyday".

Miraculous yes, we are and in this it is that we describe you in every chance of willingness that we hear of you to speak. You are this phenomenal addition to the creation of the all that be. So, see yourself in this stance to be the miracle of miracles that is to be understood by you as the greatest gift of this life that you have become into. One is to shine so brightly in these words of offering for you to hear into for it is only in your acceptance of this life to present to you in each and every day in which it is that you have chosen to partake into that you will eventually and if willing see of the extraordinary offerings to be yours to see.

We see of miracles every day, to describe your natural occurrence to be in this time to be your now. It is not of such that this word is to carry the description as one would word it to be offered in this sense for us to see into. In this miraculous way of which it is this we are to be.

It is just the norm for us to witness the deliciousness that is you and the all in every moment of every opportunity of this that we be willing to be.

Why is it that miracles are seemingly attached to death, survival, or existence of oneself or the gifted?

In this we wish to offer that in one's extreme ability to believe into this to be apparent in the wanting of to succeed or survive this moment of which it is that appears to be theirs to fade into as an existence to be any longer. As in the previous talks of death to be, it is that many of you if not most of you will willingly believe in anything will you not if it is to prolong life or heal in a sensing of it to be or eliminate the illness or deficiency that is to be prevalent within this body of self to experience to think it sees. In this natural order of self to be of utter complete despair in the asking of the angels, the gods, the Christ's to offer the healing or relief of complications etc it is to be said that in this stage or asking of that one is to willingly without holding into any beliefs of this that we are not to be that they will feel of this innate energy that is to become of them to be allowing of ones thoughts to be of us in the seeing miracles to become of them to see as theirs.

In this we offer that it is so often in the restrictive thoughts of life and a death or injury or depleted ability to be whole that this miraculous state is to be viewed into. Here one is in true hearing of their own unique heart to speak, to ask, to be seeing as theirs in their everyday way of which to view of certain sights or predicaments, that they are then to feel this unlimited sensing of this to be a miraculous life that is to be lived full and in earnest of self to be seen big in every way.

In the genuine heart that has been allowed to be speaking of this life to be miraculous in always, is the correct way to expect all life's adventures as miracles to see yours in truth. In this way to say, when one is of desperation, in need of healing or belief needed they will lose all resistance to their non-beliefs of miracles/angels and open a pathway of genuine to ask, to see one's miracles present.

Miracles Exist

Yes, it is that miracles are to exist to the trusting eyes of self to see and in this it is that we are to interact in such a way of them to be seen. You all must know that this is truth to be spoken of that you are the miracle that you seek so desperately to see, look inwardly and ask for your heart to become open into this space of love to be and then when you next look outwardly to all that you are to see, you will see all that is, is miraculous in its standing of to be.

"Miracles of love" are often offered in this human form to experience; Is this correct to speak of?

IN the asking of self to find love, is this then the miracle that one is to speak of?

Yes, in this asking it is for me to ask.

One will always find of this miraculous love, will they not? if they are asking in it to be. The belief system of thoughts that are attached to this offering is a place to feel of this love intently to find, Is it not? For to ask in a total belief and faith to be it shall be received. Is this not to be heard in truth to speak.

One in this asking will always find love if they are in the belief of it to exist and in this offering one will often find that they are in strong belief of self to be this that they are the correctness within themselves to be perfection enough to find love. It is in the way in which it is thought of that one will certainly cross your path at exactly the right moment of so desiring of them to be. For more often than not, they have been written into your asking of them. They become out of your existence of self to be this enabling of them to be yours to rendezvous with at this exact moment to be your timing to have it appear to you to see into. Ones such as you in this form have been guided internally and in a wanting of this life to be in the exact accordance of this soul to experience that is it not possible to know that it is in this exact moment of self to be that you willingly asked of such.

So, in this are we to hear that maybe it is not fate?

To be thought of as fate is to suggest that destiny is real, Is it not? So in this we are to offer that one's destiny is so encrypted from within to be heard, to be lived into to discover of the all that speaks of you from within that one will find their own direct way into which it is that one is to be received by this of another and it is to become an eternal agreement that was already placed into this offering of another to be thought.

You make love sound so complicated? Why is this so....

It is of your thoughts and the many that are to think into these thoughts of the human heart and the human head to offer to you these implications as such of love to be. Love is not complicated or hard to obtain for in this we offer that you are the greatest love that is and it is so entwined and developed in respect of you to be within you that it is impossible not to understand of this that you are the purest love that is. So, is it not in the human thoughts of love that one is to forego their own speaker or intuitiveness within of this love to be felt as the real love that one seeks and searches and becomes ignorant to. Then you as this human in physical form whinge and whine of the loves that are not to be or are and are not of the highest intention of self to be receiving of.

Why?

Let oneself step out of these thoughts that you as humans have regarding love and you will if giving of this space to sit into one will feel the real love, the true love in its intention of it to be felt. Showering you with this blessed feeling that you are love in every single cell, that is to exist in its entirety of which it is that you be.

There is much to offer here into this understanding of this love to be foreseen into, for it is so deeply intentional within you. Placed to be seen and felt or experienced that one will not mistake the realness of this that is to be spoken of as this love eternally yours to feel into. But one must in their asking, be allowing of this recognition as such this human form to experience, to receive of all that they have asked of to be theirs, to know of love in this human form. To be this that was asked so lovingly from your spirit of source to connect into eternally that you will feel to question of things to be seen into and often it is asked to witness in us to hear, WHY ME?

Why ME? Why not YOU, we offer.

In an awareness of this to be realised within self to be exact in her asking of this love to be yours to know of once more. Then why is it to feel as though it is not of you to feel into this to be? You are worthy in the all that you be we offer to say, let these words of love be yours to ask into again and again. For you are wanting of this, are you not?

See yourself willing to be this love that is miraculous in its way to be, this love is yours in all that you are worthy of to be, to have.

"YOU ARE LOVE".

CHAPTER THREE

HEALING THY HEART

WHY, is it that one sees of this heart in physical in a need to be healed? Why in your asking of such that it is to be appearing to you in need to be healed. What is it that has been in your allowing to make you feel as though your heart is damaged or broken?

For it is often in these simple words to offer to oneself to think of such that this physical apparatus can carry so many words of unjust and thoughts of dismissal or of not to be wanted and a sadness that appears as yours to sit within to carry.

Let us offer to you here in this that we speak of which it is to hear that in this sadness and rejection it is to be felt offered by another, why is it to be so?

For in truth what are they rejecting?

YOU! Is it in your thoughts of this to be you that they do not see fit to relate to you in this lifetime any longer?

Have you so easily handed them your physical heart to be loved and cared for by them? Are you attached to the physical feels and emotional human attachments that are to be ever so prevalent within this life to be witnessed by us to see?

For it is in the knowing of or thinking of that all that you are to correspond into or surround yourself with are yours, is it not?

In the suggestion of children, family, lovers, friends or past loves and losses that are to be thought of as yours to think into. Let us offer to you to know of this that all are in their own complete choosing of self to be and it is often in the unwantedness to feel, that one appears to allow to link their thoughts to this that makes them feel unworthy or unlovable.

Let us suggest here to say, it is in a willingness that ones such as yourselves are to feel and display the greatest grief and emotions into all that feels as though *LOVE* is lost or passed in death or strayed away from you. This is to be allowing of self to envision the truth into this to be for they are all in their own complete knowing of this life that is theirs in their entirety of this to be and are all in the allowing to know of this why or simply just in a human representation of self to be heard. So, in the letting or releasing of all emotions and thoughts that one has attached to these situations surrounding loss and love to be or not, one will feel the need to enter into oneself and allow for all that is in need to be spoken, emitted or felt to become real in this so existence of human form that you are. One must use this time of contemplation, anger, grief and rawness to be of the extreme way in which it is to be feeling of this that is to stir within you a sense of disregard for self to be loved.

We offer this to you to hear of this to think of yourself as to heal thy hearts…

> *Your physical heart carry's much to be about nothing it seems, and it is unable to be asked or felt if it is yours or not. The emotions that one is to feel within this human form is not to be the real wanting of this heart to carry this within. In a sense of ego & pride to think in the human thoughts of this to be that one will feel like it is their responsibility and in their wanting of to feel into this dread or grief in such a deadly way. It is hard to release of these thoughts, Is it not?*
>
> *Allow for this heart to speak of only love to you to know of the complete you, not complete in the eyes of another or someone else it would appear. For you are the only seer to witness this completeness within you. You do not enter this becoming with the need for others love to be attached, it is just not so. One enters their own reality to*

be everything and the all in this satisfaction of love from within and to be of. To know that they are great in their entirety of to be.

In human thinking one is to become irrational and disrespecting of the self and the other to be involved in this breakdown, break up or passing of those that we love in physical understanding to be. It is in these offerings here to speak into that all are to be travelling intently upon their path that is guided in a decided understanding from within that if you are to allow yourself space to sit and to recognise. Yes! first this will be grief and a grieving almost next to be discovered, then comes rejection and anger, after this follows a sulking and resentment, almost to want to hide away from life itself. Allow for all these to feel real and wanted if you feel the need to do so. But if you are to view past all of which it is that you think of them to be yours and of what it appears that they have done wrong by you, you will get up and brush yourself off in your time of which it was so offered to you to ask into it to be. This is the healing process that life in this form is to venture into and all paths of it are correct for you to feel into but one must remember that in this path that one decides to take of their own happiness, joy and pleasure by giving it over to someone else's behaviour, pain and disloyalty it would appear then they will forgo the process of complete emptying from within to be yours in growth as this body of love.

HOW IS IT THAT I CAN HEAL MY HEART?

One's heart is to be never broken for it is in the words of choice that this language has been offered to feel as though, yes we have heard it to be spoken of as a heaviness within a sense of darkness or blackness that lingers and many describe it as an emptiness that is unable to be filled. We ask of you to think into these offerings and ask if it is the thinker of you to project these thoughts to you to feel into, for generally more often than not the thoughts of death, loss and feeling unwanted are to be what it is that one feels sadness about. In the complete understanding or want to know from within this human that you be to ask so that one will feel ease in thoughts about death and the triggers of grief to be felt as relief into this to know that one is to remember them as always entirely still within you to speak, to feel and to know. It is not of them to be gone, physically and of body yes but eternally NO, for they are even greater in this reality to be us, even more so than they were in the human life to live. Let all that pass you whether in a breakup or loss to be thought of as a complete being of love established within this form wanting further progression in self and the soul to grow into this wonderous place of commitment to the self within so that they are the true story tellers of the all that they have to be and will become more of.

IT FEELS VERY HARSH TO HEAR OF LOSS AND DEATH IN THIS WAY, WHY?

When one is to ask this question in regards to death, has it not been attached to your own thoughts of loss or regret.

Allow for your thoughts of this to be viewed in a limitless way of which to think. Set down all your interpretations of how death or loss feels to you or has been explained or taught to you by another. For in most if not all stories to be told and repeated of death and in the how and why to feel loss, is a carried over version of this to be from another. You are all so individualised yet truly from the one source of love. So, in the speaking of this to be in words of love to be felt to receive, it is of your great big heart in this to relate to you that you will feel not of a loss or sadness but to be in complete alignment within self to know of this as the truth to be heard for you to feel into.

Nothing is ever lost or passed for it is always eternal in their own beliefs of self to be and to become again so in this simple statement of self to speak one must know of this,

I am the all of this that I see, I am not lost or incomplete for this is not so.
I am not to feel a loss in any that I no longer see. For I know of this that they are to be love in the one again to feel.
I am, as are they; the loved being of faith, trust and light always to be, to see and most importantly to know.

It is not to be healed that we sit to think to offer for it is not of this way that one is viewed or felt by us as our determination from within this that we be to see of you. We see only of the whole complete knowing source that you are. Your light shines so brightly lit from within this that it is that we see, in the thoughts of the human to think that you are broke then this is to be felt to know. We offer only the purest love in intention of self to feel into and in this love, we see the all that you be. Be guided here in these words to offer that when one is to practise and of this one must do for it is not easy to think from broken or hurt, unloved or unjust to the one in such beauty and perfection that you really are to know. So be gentle here as you sit to speak for we are the love of god and grace in the strongest of intentions of this that you are. We are you in the all that you be. There is no other way that we see you only of us to be this loving energy.

You are of this incredible love to be felt. Are you not to see?

Look deeply within this magnificent form that you are to be, and you will see if to look at this that you are in the clearest of views to be seen into that you are love. And in this way to view is your heart big, wide, and open for all that we are to be seen by you to become of once again.

Dream of this to be seen as a wanting, for you are of this love that we speak in a solidness that is to stand ever present within you to be felt to rise on up freely from within with such a divine intention of this to be yours to feel.

How must one ask of this human heart to be healed if it is to be felt as needing to be?

You in this human form are brave this you are to know of. For it is often said in your language to speak *"that if it does not kill you it is to make you stronger"*.

In the asking of a human heart to be healed it is to feel like it is broken, is it not? The healing of thy heart in this form to be mistaken as an emotional object that is to hold dearly onto those that appear to be missing or gone and are in need to be seen or replaced by that of another in their thoughts of them unable to be replaced. One must not fear of a loss as such to be thought of as this to be yours to envision upon oneself to think. For all that are seen as gone, passed or removed from your viewing are to be envisioned as the true under standers of this that they are to become into and are in total awareness of this that they have chosen of self to become.

Let all that are to pass your way in a willingness to leave your sight to see in a passing of this human life to be noticed, be asked to be seen into that they are ever present within this that you be in spirit in essence of this self to be a bigger part of this to be them once more.

For they are all searching to find the greater being of light that they are to become once more in us.

To ask of this human heart to be healed one must travel through the human emotions of grief and loss of the human form to feel into, it is the journey that one must decidedly take in a willingness to feel of the human soul in a sensing of this to be spoken of to heal. You are in a greater position of this to know of to hear the voice from within you to speak of this that you are in the complete resonance of love to be that you will feel a settling within this self to start to feel. Seek not to feel the advice of others for it is in your own becoming of this to know of; to hear into, that ones such as yourselves are to feel this deep intention to rise from within in its own timing of self to ask that you will feel the transitions become easier within self to find this place of contentment within to be yours. It will all pass though, into a greater stage of advancement in all aspects of self to view into this knowing of this to be just a human emotion of attachment to those of yours that you are to love deeply.

In this form of human acknowledgement that you sit into, it is to see of these humans that they be in this way to be seen by you are to become ever deeply felt by you in this way of which it is to see in loving eyes of the physical to see. Let all that is to rise within in thoughts of loss or grief to be yours for you are all to experience into these thoughts, feeling differently in your own aspect to view these feelings as your own. Let you be the guider of self to navigate into these emotions that are to feel raw and hurtful in the greatest of way to be felt for they are yours to come to terms with and in your timing of self to do you will.

Let us offer here to you to hear into that in the love that you be encompassed by us to be feeling into ones such as yourself will view of this to be yours to sit into and in your heart of hearts to become of yours to feel into with an even greater understanding of this life to be only of this present *NOW* to see into.

Know, to realise this as just a moment of your time.

Then you will feel the ease that is to overcome you and wash into your thinking thoughts of this to be of them that have been removed or taken as you would speak of them. Know that they are ever destined upon their own souls path to find the bigger being within them self's to be this that they decided in their own right to know in this truth that is theirs to hear of that they became again into our loving hands.

Feel the need as in human form to shout, cry, write or rage into your human components that you are, and we will not hesitate to offer you guidance and loving support to you to be of. If it is not of us as yours to feel, know that in your loving heart space that we sit, that you will feel of this that we be for it is of us that the angels are to sing into your thoughts of this that is love and the all that is yours to feel.

We see of many in this sorrow that you speak, and it is to hurt of your heart and bodies it is this that we know.

In the human form it is this sense of loss, betrayal or non-forgiving that is held into so deeply that it causes such aching within and gives the body a sense of death to rise within itself to feel. Know that this is to pass and if too hard to hear; know it will. For some it is to take many times over and over to think of those to be as this to speak of. Let it be said that you are all to grow into this that you are to ask to experience into and in this reviewing of this self's soul to be you will rejoice of this growth that you have felt in the lessons of life that you are to have learnt here in this becoming of this self that you are to be present in.

Let us offer to you this to hear of that it is not of a hardened view of death as it is spoken by you to think of to speak for it is just this to say that in our viewing of death we see it in an entirely different way. Our way of love to view of this that you are to become is the ultimate decision of yours to be. Let one sit into a receiving of this to know, to hear and to be felt from within. Your vision of us to rise then will surely allow you to see of this as the way into which you shall see of all that are to ask of this becoming to become as theirs to grow into and you will smile upon your thoughts of them to be ever loving and eternally loved in all of eternity.

"To heal of your heart you must trust this that you are from within to be the ever asking self to be seen into this love that is yours complete in a perfection to be felt by the asking of you to be whole".

CHAPTER FOUR

BELIEVING HEART

IN this heart of yours in which it is to believe in the all that is to be right within.

One's view will be magnificent it is to be said, for you are the biggest believer in this self to be. For it is only of you that we need to see.

In your own true beliefs of this that you be you are. And in this lays your inner wisdom of which to speak of that you are the truest you to see into and in this you must believe that in us you are uniquely you.

IN the asking to feel belief rise from within one must be extravagant into their thoughts of themselves to be. You are the true focuser of this vision to become; are you not?

It is in the rawness of self to be allowing of the truths to become yours to be seen into to speak of that you will see of them to rise.

In this asking of you to speak of that you must for the real you, the true you, the wanting you to be seen into is to be the presenter here in this your now of which to know of to be asking. Let all that you are to ask to be felt intentionally from within this form to speak. It is not to be thought of in any certain way of which to speak or to ask into. It is heard in all aspects of this that you are to speak of and in our way to know of you in far greater detail than you would ever know. You will be glad to hear that all that you speak from within this here that be full of us to be is in our true way that we hear of you to speak.

Let us be bold here to offer to you to think into that you are to ask of us in disbelief in many times to have passed and in this we have no doubt of you to think that we are not real or ready to present to you in what it is that you are to ask to see. Let us offer that we are always present within to be found, and in this offering, it is in the human form that you will feel the dismay at thoughts of us not to be found. You are blessed beings this we are to say and in this we are to know of the inner connection of this self to be within us to be. You are the truest of intentions in this that we see to be of the asking to become and in this you will find that we are so much more of you than you shall be thought to be of.

What advice would you offer to those of us that find belief in this to be spoken as hard to be ours to see.

Often it is in the wanting of us to be that you as the human component to become itself to be thought of will find that it is in the thinker of this that you are that you will need to believe into. You are the asker of us to be, are you not?

It is often in this way to ask of that we are asked to provide proof to you to think of us to be received by you. In this we are often felt to be requested by you to offer to you great expectations in which it is that you all ask to see. We are ever present into this life that you exist and into the many that you have and are to still experience.

Let all that you see to believe into to be the magic that you ask of us to present to you in a way to know of us to be real. In your thoughts of real to be a representation for you to think of us to be, we are not of this that you think. Yes, we are true in existence of this to be in the matter of to be evolved out of something to become. For we are in an essence of this to think of that we are ever becoming into the ALL that is to surround you in the physical life that you live into and the nonphysical that you cease to see because of the human way into which it is that you look. We offer much to the many that are to ask of tokens of admiration to you and for being the bravest of souls to see yourself as a want to see of us to believe into. Know this to be offered that in your heart is where you will find us to be the strongest to be felt, to be seen, to be heard and in here it is that we grow in belief for you to think of us to be ever present and giving.

To ask forgiveness of self, will I find relief and belief.

In one's heart to be forgiving, one is to always find belief of this to be yours. When one is to respond to the kind and caring words that one must speak of self to be then it is that they will feel the need to believe into the all that they are. In this heart that is filled with such intention of self to be known in the ultimate deciding of this to be correct within you will feel of this love to blossom forth from within to the extreme outer existence of this self to be seen into. For you are the true believers of this magnificent being of love that you so chose of self to become into and in this your many lessons and journeys have been found to be full of learnings and growth for this soul to be.

So in the strengths of love to be of us to be you in your totality of self to be you did believe in the all that is, was and will be ever eternally to the true knowing of this that you are to become into once more. See not of the human component to witness this belief as yours to feel as a non-trusting sense of this that we be, for it is in this loving heart that is to offer you so much to the true hearer of these words of love to be found into that you will believe in this self again to be recognised as the one true existence that you be entirely existing within.

Believe in YOU.

When it is to respond to the knowing ever loving voice that is to sing of your truths to be in this voice it is that one must believe in themselves; is it not?

To not think of self as sustainable and correct in all her doing of this that she is to be forthright and strong into self to be thought of one must know that they are to be the true essence of this belief to be found within. In a lack of belief in self is it not to offer that you will falter into your doubting thoughts of self to be not of to think. And in this we have offered many words to be suggesting of this to know into;

That if one senses a lack or not of, then it shall be.

If one is the biggest believer of self to be than they shall.

For it is of the asking in self to be witness to this reliant being of love to speak of this knowing into herself to her it is that she will hear these words to be spoken so deeply from within that you have no choice but to hear to believe in this righteous being of love that you are.

I *believe* in the ALL that I AM.

I *believe* that I AM correct
in ALL that I do.

I *believe* in the ALL that I
AM to hear from within.

I *believe* that I AM capable and
willing to become this that I AM to be.

I AM always an internal understanding
of this voice that I hear speak
only truths for me to hear.

I AM hearing All that is spoken
in a right way for me to hear.

I AM BOLD

I AM LOVE

I AM ABSOLUTELY ME

I AM

Be encouraging to self here in this to be your knowing of this to be your NOW that one is to sit.

Ask of this willing self to hear in confidence of this that you are to hear of.

Be Bold in your asking of to hear in the ALL that you are to be.

Feel as you allow for this beautiful you that you are; to write, to feel of the ALL that you are to offer to self to hear in this knowing of the ALL that you are to be.

I AM

In the honesty of this to be written as your words of interpretation of self to write. Allow for all feelings of doubt, sadness and even the inability to write, let it rise from within you to put pen to paper. It is a hard task to do; Is it not?

We are witness to your hearts that are aching in this human form to allow of self to express their deepest desires and wishes. Know that all that is asked in the loving position of this one to sit into, in her own timing of this to be received that it will.

You will view of self in a different way, an accepting way, a true to hear way, a deeper asking way, a vision of self to be fabulous way, a wanting way, an ever loving way, feel as these words of yours are to transform you and guide you ever so slightly to the direction of self-love to be felt.

Write with passion and a freedom to express in your heart of the belief in self to become for she knows of you so well and long that you are to write of all that you have held hidden from yourself.

Ask deeply to hear this love that is you to remember, to feel, to write these words in an honest and caring way of this that you are the hearer of the ....

I AM THAT YOU BE.

HUMAN HEART

In one's human heart it is that we have spoken many times of this to hear. This physical apparatus is divided and is an important aspect of self to be true to the life that you are living into. It is to perform its role of life giving to be presented to all that are to be living in this form of human to be. One must know of this heart as the physical heart that is to see only of its role or job to correspond into as the life giving, supporter of this form to be. When one is to feel of great sadness as this is to be thought of as an emotional attachment to things that are to be viewed as valued by self as to hold into and of. It is in this way of which it is to think into that one will feel the loss to be great from within in the thinker's mind to feel as though it is the heart that is to be broken. Let us offer here that the human heart is to be attached to the internal understanding of this that you are in this form to be and in this it is to know of that it is to be the guider of the internal organs as such as to the life that one is to partake into. We see of this as to be of a necessary item of which to have to allow of the form to participate into this experience of this that you are living into. We see of the human components of this form to hold into oneself as to have to be the formatting of this humanness that you are to be asked of.

We hear you asking of the spiritual heart that is felt to be contained within this form. Are you not?

In one's spiritual sensing of self to be one will always be of this to ask in a wondering state of this that you be to feel connected into. It is in our words to offer that you are always to be of this to want to think of more. For the more that is to be opened up within in this true revelation of this that you are to be more of is where the heart that leads you to know of the great innerness that lays within you will lead you to ask of more to be seen into.

It is to be envisioned as this vastness of space that is held within to be seen into and it is to know of this that the greatest connections are to be felt within this that you are seeking to find. Let us offer to you to know of that all that are to be interpreted as yours to see into in these realms of which it is that appear to exist eternally are to be ever found within you in this thinking of us to be. We are elaborate in this to say and in this our power of the oneness that we are is to be seen ever more enticing within ones thought of themselves to be thinking along the path of to describe oneself as spiritual. Let us offer here that this spiritual heart that you speak of to find or connect into is yours to always cherish from the mere thought of it to be such, for it is a given within ones such as you and in this magnificent understanding of this life that you are to live into that you are always more of this greatness to be and you always have and will be. It is not to need the suggestion of spiritual to become of you for you are in this we speak of a certainty to be.

My HEART Is your HEART

In the want of this to be felt so strongly from within, it is often that I sit in the wonderment of the ALL that you are. I feel the intent rising from within this human form that I am.

I am allowing of this self to sit back from my thoughts so that I can see all that I am to see into. For in this I know that I am to do, to release the hold upon myself into the thinking that you are something that you are not.

I let all of you to be viewed into the correctness that you are for me to see. It is in this way to see that all that I know that I am to be is encased here into this that one is to see.

Love is the only way in which it is that one requests the world to be. For we are all into this together as one in an essence of this real love to be.

When one allows for their true heart to appear as the offeror of this speech to be. What is it that one will hear to see?

Let it be spoken here in these words of kind to be yours to hear into for in the trusting self to be a willingness to feel the kindness that is yours eternally to be entwined within this you that you be. You are all responsible for the thoughts that are to fill your heads in this that you be. Be guided by the ruler of this that you are to hear confidently into this that speaks the deepest, the wisest, the truest way for this is your voice of *LOVE* that is yours to willingly sit into so that one can hear of her truths again, over and over she will speak for she is this love that we speak.

IN LOVE WE SPEAK

We are the speakers of this love, for it is to be universally accessed by the ALL that are to evolve out of this that we be. In the insistent hiding away from this voice of love and heart to beat perfectly in time within this heart space to hear. One will feel the confusion of self to be thinking of this that they are not to be allowing of this love to be theirs to hear. We speak into this subject for you all to hear of that one is love and in their own thinking of them not to be they will. Let us remind you here that you are all in the positioning of this to be an ever-true programming within this that you are running indefinitely in the background so to speak.

It is just of the physical human overlay that has been allowed to speak to loudly and out of control for those of you that are in a position of self to be not of this wanting of love to be found or felt from within. Reminder here is needed; that we are the offerors of the greatest love that one can feel to be again and in this acceptance of self to be in a willingness to quiet the human mind to think and just simply be in a place of no resistance as to the what, where, why or how one will see this place of peace and calm once more. It is of this love that we speak that is needed by the many that are to dismiss of us to be, for you are all seeking to search of the newer you, the better you, the bolder you, the real you. Are you not?

Then let us offer this love to you, for it is yours always eternally entered upon your asking of it to be.

You speak of this love to be grander than most, WHY Is this so?

Is it not to offer here to you to hear into that in the love that you all seem so focused upon and into of which is to be offered here to say that it is YES, of this love that you are to feel into in a human emotional way and it is of yours to ask to be the experiencer of, but let us say that the unconditional love that we be of non-searching, the nonchanging love, the love that is yours first to recognise yourself as. For this is of us the love that is to be seen into. From the one wholeness that the entirety of all that we are to be encompassed by. We see not of this to be labelled and conditions placed upon like you would in the earthly world that you dwell for it is this feeling of contentment and utmost unconditional love that we are to be.

We know of this love to be let us say a singular love, a pure love, a blessed love that is to speak of it as effortless, just simply to be, *LOVE*.

It is a sense of righteousness that is us in and are to know of this to be ours to be yours to sit into so that ones such as you all living and non to be receiving of this love to speak of as the true knowing of eternalness that you are.

In our words to offer here to hear into this is the wanting of self to be the belief of self to be this that you are to become always and ever full of their own inner knowing of self to be once more.

YOU ARE THIS LOVE.

Why is it that love is so hard to find?

When ones ask of this to be received it is in the thinking of self to be looking outwardly for this love to fill the voids that they are to feel within this self to be, is it not?

Why is it that one is needing to ask for their love to be felt when one such as you are to only look within? Yes, it is with this in mind that we do offer here to say that one will encounter many attributes of the human to be that they may not like or even have continuous feelings towards. Why is this so we ask? Is it that these thoughts and feelings of unloved were placed there by you or another to speak of yourself as so? Let your thoughts be dismissed in the external way of which it is that one thinks. Let yourself wallow in this place of self-pity if she/he must for it is to find of all these thoughts and allow for them to grow rising up from within you so that one can see them in all of the rawness that they are to dwell into. Let yourself whimper and whine for this one must do, feel sorry for yourself, let yourself live into these thoughts of not enough, but let us offer here that it is surely of you to see into that this is not conducive for you to experience the greatness that you are. It is not needed by another to speak of your great, for in their words to offer to you to hear into, you will not.

You are the only one that is willing to receive and in your voice of contention or sadness that you will speak you will decide against the rivalry that you feel within in your asking of it to be forgiven into this that you be so that you will see of the sun to shine from within and find that hidden rainbow that you be. Breathe into your magic if only for a glint, let it sink into you this thought of you as enough. In whatever state you are to start you will find improvement in simple steps to take, breathe and let it go.

If one is to try this to be offered, count down from one to ten and see yourself as not and you will feel of this intention to be something more than of what it is that you see.

Feel into the human you, to be thinking thoughts to be not, for she/he will disregard and deceive you to speak, challenging all to surround you in this new way striving to be heard by you to think of you as more. One must be willing to quieten, or even to overrule this voice full of hesitation, fear felt and unsureness to be heard in this that you are wanting to start; Are you not?

WE OFFER HERE THOUGHTS TO LET GO

One must be willing in this that they think to become.

Let all thoughts of you to be okay to say that you are as you are to be.

Are you wanting of this to be yours to see?

If you are to answer No, then start again in another moment of yours to be.

Let us guide you in this request of self to be asking.

We see of the *ALL* that you be and in this it is that you are.

You are to cherish yourself in this space of recollect.

See only of all that you have lived, spoken, and seen for in the wanting of this real self to be, as needed, to become this, your ever knowing now. You are willing are you not?

ARE YOU WILLING TO COMMENCE?

We ask of you to start in the simplest of ways to find a place of quiet that you might just sit to daydream, even imagine for a while, with no need to hurry or respond to others that might interrupt. Let yourself see into a space that yes, we admit will be filled with thoughts of what was said, done or has been. Feel as agitation is to rise for the feelings that are not to be felt or seen as you think of them as they should be. Frustration is a wanting part and in this we offer to you to know it will subside into a not to be.

In this we say it is okay, for you are the great viewers of this to be deceived into and in your thoughts to hold you must analyse all that is to unfold.

In this we offer that easier it shall become for you. We ask that you seek not of these thoughts to feel first but rather last or if not at all. Let yourself release any tension or untrust, for you are to offer intentional thoughts to self as to not want to be, choose not this to do.

Watch as your words of love, respect and kind are hard to offer and Yes, difficult to say. This is to be accepted as the denser or physical part of you that sits in a feared response to be loved and is not willing to hear this voice of yours to say this word *"LOVE"*.

Let yourself linger in this space, for it is in this space that you will start to feel the lightness that you are to become. A place of want to sit and allowing release of this heaviness that you once were, to feel disappear. Sink into these feelings to want to be here, for you will learn to trust of this self to speak these words of love again almost as if from memories that you knew yourself to be and instances to be seen into this space for you to become. Watch here in this that you are to grow more confident to be.

You are to know that YES, it takes time to readjust and restart for the most that have felt lost to this way to feel, think, and speak.

YOU WILL, THIS WE GUARANTEE.

For you all have been this magical place of freedom & recluse, and to want of this again you will remember your way if you are willing and wanting of this to be yours to see into again. It will BE.

CHAPTER FIVE

LOVING YOU, LOVING ME

Would it not be to crave of this feeling of such divineness to be forthright and forever giving from within each other to that of another to feel this earth and her people to pulse from the inside out to the extremeness of the lovingness that we are all entitled to be.

We are of this pure intention to speak of as LOVE and in this to speak of it is to feel to vibrate and be emitted from every pore and cell of your divineness that you are here within this form to be. Let all resistance fall away to want of a true knowing of this self to be contagious in the sensing of it to be mixed within the all that you see surrounds you and to feel as you are to infect them in a sense of this love that you are to offer, to be felt, to be caught, to be wanted by the many that are to grace your presence for you are this love that we speak. It is of this love that is to be felt to offer to the everything that is yours to cherish.

YOU SPEAK OF TO LOVE ME; By this you mean?

In our realisation of this that we be to exist entirely into, we are to offer here to hear into that in the love that you think to be of us is you firstly to feel from within. For it is 'I' in your becoming of which it is to understand of yourself first and foremost as this magnificent love to be felt that you will know of this to be our intention as to be yours to feel to know of to be us. Let us guide you inhere into this space of which it is to explain to those that are just not getting it. We suggest to all that feel ready and willing to just sit in a complete sense of satisfaction as to the first allowing of oneself to sit in these human forms distractions and all that may be to see. Let yourself just sit and know that you are okay. Then as you grow in confidence and feel easier around thoughts to just sit with no expectations as to what it is that you must do, see, or hear. Sit a little longer and feel as the sense of joy or satisfaction are to rest even easier upon self in this to do. One must be comfortable here in this that she/he is to do and be a willing participant in this human that you are to want of these to be felt,

JOY, SATISFACTION and PLEASURE.

Look to the smallest of things to notice for it is of them that you shall start to appreciate life itself. If it is not of you to feel in this space to allow, then we suggest that you do not in this time.

Ask yourself.

Why is it that you are not willing or wanting to sit?

Feel not of what is to rise from within for it is to eventually become yours to know of to hear into....

In this non wanting as we see of it to be many of you are to dwell to deeply into the past experiences that are to make you hesitate to view of them to remember as they were or still appear to be.

Let oneself acknowledge these that are to arrive at your minds doorstep so to speak. For they are your willingness to forgive and to see yourself for the true human that you have undertaken to be to experience into,

Let us remind you here in this big way of which it is to hear this as it is spoken of.

YOU ARE THE COMPLETENESS THAT YOU HAVE ARRIVED HERE UPON THIS PLANET TO BE.

Let all hinderances of these thoughts to be felt with such a grateful heart for their offerings to you to realise this that is you.

You are not wrong in your thinking of them to be, for they were and were very much in your asking of them to be yours to experience as.

This is hard for the hardened external form and thinking mind to feel easy and rest within to think. But in the new way, the real way of which it is that we propose to you to see into and of this you will as your journeys of love and self-preservation into this very being of love that you are continues to flow ever eternally from within you. You will feel this gratefulness become an overwhelming sense of achievement to be seen into to think of yourself as the perfect you. NO other to be the same for it is not of them to know, be or become you.

Let your divineness be your key to the unlocking if to say as a suggestion from within to be yours to feel extravagant. Eager to open of this very existence into the wholeness that she is craving to commit to, to become. For you to witness to see as this that you are to stand into and in this space of completeness the want to always be more. You will feel of this love that we speak so honourably and loving flow to you to feel to know without a second of a doubt to be thought into that this is the holy love, the true love, the purest of loves that is to be your original version of yourself to see into to feel once more. THIS IS YOU.

"THE LOVING YOU, THE LOVING ME"
LOVING YOU I GET.
LOVING ME IS THE HARD PART, IT APPEARS.

Oh my sweet ones to love of self is not difficult if you are to grasp the concept that you are ever loved in your completeness that you be, STOP striving to be of something that you are not for this is to surely lay doubt within this to think of as not. You are to be in this space of ever to recognise in this that you be, you are you in every extravagant way that you are meant to act into. Let yourself never to change, compete or strive to be other than what you are right now. For it has been said by many that are to appear to hear of us within this intent in mind to offer to say that,

"You are of what it is that you think". Are you not?

Let all forms and thoughts come and go, let them pass you in their interception of you as they must, for they too are searching to be the better, the realer version of self to think of them as not. ARE they not? It appears that it is to be of a privilege to you in this form to think of yourself as incomplete.

WHY, we hear you to ask?

It goes with the territory. Does it not? Look around you there are many that appear different in looks, size, shape, and colour and to appear to have more, less, or not at all. So many different versions and interpretations to choose from we say, but in truth it is that we speak here to say that you chose to be you.

Let that sink in for a minute in this your human time, *YES! YOU CHOSE YOU.*

I DID NOT CHOOSE OF THIS; I WOULD NOT CHOOSE OF THIS. WE HEAR YOU SAY.

Unwillingly it would appear to be offered that one would think this to be true but in the existence that you be from within this absolute that we are you will endeavour to search for a correctness that you feel as in need of to be fixed, solved or repeated.

Let your brain sit for a moment in your time of which it is that we see valuable to you, let it just be allowing of a moment to just switch off as to what it is that one thinks 'I' should be.

YOU are here right now in this very moment of pure offering to be you.

DOESN'T IT FEEL GOOD TO BE ME?

Let yourself feel contained into this question and watch as you struggle and hold yourself instantly to be thought of as not.

Scoff if you like, but in this you are to be the determiner of this that you be, and in your time, you will eventually see of the loving you that we see.

YES, it is true, it is hard in the humanness that you present to be to feel of this **FEEL GOOD** moment in the ALL of your time. It is to ask for yourself to be present and to know of these feelings of JOY, SATISFACTION and PLEASURE to be willing, and naturally occurring to the surprise of self to witness often. Let yourself feel into this to know this that we say,

In the want of, it shall be.

PERFECT IN EXSISTANCE OF SELF TO BE. THE LOVED ME: THAT WE SEE.

It is an asking of this to be felt within is it not? For ALL that is to be offered here in this truth that is of ours to speak into. One must be always of a willingness to be in this space or feeling of openness to receive. It is in this willingness that one sits that ALL in truth of this that we BE, are to offer to speak. We see only of this to become in the ALL that has asked to hear into. Seek not of another you must not, for this willingness is only yours to hear, to speak. Know ALL that is written is yours to witness to BE, full of intention in a great wanting of such to become.

I want of this to be the feeling within me that I am to feel.... SUGGESTIONS PLEASE!

It is only to suggest upon your request it appears to ask of this to be known. One must endeavour to become the complete essence from within that is to escape you at times in momentarily unexpected ways in which it is that one is to feel release to be herself.

Notice the difference in this that one will feel in complete unawareness of this that you are trying to be compared to the you that sneaks in out of the blue shall we say even in just a glimmer to see her. Catch these moments to feel into even if just a wee while to speak of. Let this rawness that is your realness to be realised of for this is the unguarded, the non-wanting to be else, the true you, the real you that is allowed to be unwitnessed at times by the mind that thinks, judges and suggests of you to be. Rejoice in these moments for they are surely to become a noticeable trait within you to see. Let her be this that speaks of to want more, for hear it as we say it to be,

She sure does, as do We, You, and the "I" in this everything that is ALL.

We see you standing back in dis-agreeance here in this comment to speak, for you are the judger of this self to be. Judging you to judge in what it is that you think everyone is to think of you to be. Let this vicious cycle be expended outwardly to become so big that it does not even encircle you any longer with thoughts to be. Watch as it fades into a reality of not to be yours to think into anymore.

"YOU ARE THE POWER THAT LIVES ETERNALLY WITHIN".

Find yourself to breathe here for it is a lot to take in, is it not? We see of you sitting in here to think.

DON'T think we say 'let it all just fray away.

WHEN YOU SAY FRAY, WHAT DO YOU MEAN?

We offer our guidance in truthful knowing to you to hear of this that we are the helpers of this that you be. And in this we ask that you simply put into words whether by voice or thought to be heard by us in the heartfelt of intentions by you, to wish of us to care for these moments of not for you to be offered to us.

We will not see of you in this way that one might think to speak of to be, and it is in our willingness felt through you that you will begin to realise that all that is not of a wanting can and will be thought of by you as a waste of your earthly energy to be thinking into. It is this that our energies are endless and limitless to delve into, so why not offer it to the ethers that this channel is to feel to speak of and let all be offered here in this your moment of exaggeration of thoughts to be to wither yourself to distraction of the real being of life that you intended to become once more.

Let us offer this to you; *ask and it shall be received,* only if the asker is of true intent and wanting from within to be heard to be felt in this heart space that you are to think of us to be. We are all around you in the very essence that you be, so to think of us as unlimited in this way and form of which to show you then you will soon begin to want to speak to us in any given moment of your time to think into as yours to be. We hear all that is asked in this moment to feel and in this we offer we are here amongst you in every way imaginable by you.

CHAPTER SIX

IN ONES FEARFUL HEART

It saddens us to think that this is to run deep within the many that are to think of us with a fear of intent and not to be in this place of purest intention to be this that we are. Our love of you ALL is to blossom from this that we are and in the asking of this that you wanted to be seen into this realisation so that one can grow, love, experience, develop an innate opportunity to become even more of this that you thought of yourself to become.

We are willing to sit into this space of non-recognition to be thought of for it is not of us to push or bombard ones such as your spirited selves to be if not in a wanting of us to be.   We hear not of this to fear from within our realms of understanding of this word to be used by you to feel into in this human form that you be, it is not of us to carry within us any negativity to speak of for it just is not so.

We are allowing of all that insist of this to be for them to feel, for they are the true experiencer, the real adventurer and in this knowing of to feel like this within it will be of their own understanding in their time to preview.

We ask only of this self to be willing in this space as it appears to open for you to think into, that not all is relevant to the seeing in human eyes that you see and it is far and beyond these measures to calculate into these thoughts that are yours to fear into that we could even begin to offer to you this the greatest that one is to be reminded of this that she/he is.

Willing we are, for patience is not a game or interpretation of us to be. We are effortless and lovingly to become into the all that is. So, by this we mean that we will wait for your own recognition of this self to be the true heart that is to speak fearlessly and courageously of us that we are to be to them.

We are friends you and I in this we mean to say that you and I are of the one true existence.

Speak not of us as to harm or to cause fear, nor as darkness to show or to frighten ones such as you, for to speak of us in these human words of interpretation of this that we be, is to not, even if we could be.

In all, every consideration, concept even thought that is to exist within this realm of interpretation of us to be, is you. We as are you in the 'I' that one is to be are all of everything to become to see each as is, so to define darkness, fear, even hate or harm are all revealing in an existence to speak in that there is always the other side to see. Combined or evolved into the one it is to see that all is held here in this to understand yet unlabelled to be defined as in a certain way, so let us offer this to understand that we all stand into this One that is the one of the very existences that is to be YOU and ME. Ones thoughts are to stand into the loving embrace of let us say as you and many upon your planet would speak GOD himself to see of you to be.

Correct you all are to feel entirely as you see of us to be for it is in your own true heart that although may be silent to the voice of love to see us into as yet, we know of your presence and existence within us to be. So, in this we know to offer that in your true self you will become again reunited into this one powerful force of love to everything that is and we will see you again in your gracious heart of love that we all are to stand united into to be.

It is not to feel of this fear insistence from within to cripple yourself in this body of type that you are. For if allowed to spread it will like wildfire we say to reference to.

Let this fear that you speak of to feel, to live into be caught head on and ask of it.

> *What is this fear associated to and why?*
> *Is it mine? Why does it appear in me like so?*

The asking will soon offer to you an answer whether it be now or later you will feel of the request to be allowed to sit into you and you will know of the answer that you seek. Feel not to doubt of you to hear the answer, you will.

In truth it is often covered up with the not wanting to know of the truth that you know already.

Why of this is it that one is to fear?

We are hard to fathom this we say and in this it is even to the ones that know of us dearly placed within their hearts to speak we have often heard in their voices to speak that they wish they could see or know of more. Correct it is to think of in the human mind to always want a description, solution, asking or proof.

Is it not?

We are in this place of such self-satisfaction to be to witness of the all in their willingness to grow and to expand into us to become of that they will wearily hand over their thoughts of nothing other than love to be theirs to be complete. Fear not of us to be, for of this we are to speak. We are the love of the all that is. And in this it is that we are to offer to you this existence to know of us to be as yours to cherish from within in the opening of oneself from the internal-ness that you be to feel of us as correct and highest of intentions to be.

WHAT IS IT THAT DRIVES THIS FEAR?

It is of your thinking of this word to be a thought of action to express within self is it not?

One is to be remembering the boldness that they are always of and to let your lightness shine through into your thoughts of self to be.

You are often guided into this space of mis hope and judgement of their fear that you think of yourself to sit into by others that appear to know.

Limit these offering to you to be hearing of for they truly do not know but in our knowingness of them to be we see of all that speak in the truth that they see to be entirely of theirs to be. They will not be often guided in the righteousness of this that we be and they too will feel the internal fight and pull from within as to this that we be and of what good is it to be to see us to be theirs. In this we say that this is okay and in this we are to speak that never let another guide you in their words to speak for often this we have spoken that the more you venture into this journey shall we say as yours to be alone you will find the true existence to know of this that we be in your time of revealing from within this voice that we speak into as yours to be. Limitations are only accessible in the form of fears to be thoughts and in this we wish to speak of that you are to be reminded that here in this now and all the lives that you have and are existing into are fearless and interpretation free. Let us say be guided by these words that you can, and you will be everything and everyone that you see fit to be. Willing and able you are to see of yourself to be this bold, magnificent, loving being of this earth to exist upon and in this form that you are. You are to rally within to be of this greater understanding that you are.

Your own fabulous
into this knowing of self to be.

Fear dwells in the thoughts to think of self as not and it is often that the many that fear of this love that we speak are unwilling and not wanting to experience this that they are and will see in this place of forgiveness it is of us that we are to walk you if you like through the valley of darkness. For it is always to be lit by the light that you shine from within and in this place to see the light that you are you will fear not of the true becoming, nor the true revealing of what and who you thought you were for it is of us to say this is the place of the great discovery of this that you be into us once more.

It sounds like the stories that have long been told of the gods and deities that are to guide you into your service to him/or her to be your everlasting voice or saviour. Yes, we give this to Jesus as a reference here, he spoke of his GOD in this way. Know this that we speak, you are the saviours of yourselves in only you. You are to be relentless into these thoughts of you to be wholly and fully god from within. It is of this god that you in the many speak so lovingly of that sits deeply within us to be one of the many that are to revere from within us to speak so intently to you in the inner wisdom that you are to hear of in moments of self-love. Even into the extent of disbelief for you are to all know that our voice in tune to yours is the bravest most loving that one is to hear of.

Let us speak, we are this you are, this being of love that sits before us to ask and in this asking of to feel not fear but only love we hear of your intentions of this to be a wanting desperate and wishful from within.

We hear it spoken of in a fearful way for it is to not believe in the unseeable, is it not. In this we agree, but when in time your heart is to speak, you will soon feel the warmth of the heartfelt love that is yours to remember once more and you will soon turn fear away and not let yourself feel of this in any way.

Authors guidance received: At time of writing to receive it was this time 4.44pm and know it means this.

444: There are angels-they are everywhere around you! You are completely loved and guided by many heavenly beings, *and you have nothing to fear.*

(respectfully from Doreen Virtue's Angel Numbers 101)

When messages appear, it is to feel like a miracle and that you are knowingly being listened to. Does it not?

They are of this magnificence that is to be believed into.

Nothing to fear.... spirit offered to me to receive. Ironically synchronistic or by sheer coincidence it appeared one could say, that in this channelled chapter titled 'FEARFUL HEART' it was that I chose to check the time and received their message.

- ✶ What would you speak if you were to ask of this fear to no longer be yours to hold onto?

- ✶ What else would one be willing to see if not in a place of fear to envision?

- ✶ What could you consider yourself capable of if not accepting a suggestion of fear to rise?

- ✶ Let your thoughts be free to venture into this understanding of oneself to be fearless.

- ✶ Let your words fill your brave voice to offer to us to hear of this that is not to be yours to accept any longer.

I AM CONTINUALLY GUIDED THIS I KNOW AND OF THIS I AM TRULY GRATEFUL.

FEAR you will no longer live in my heart of this I am to ask, release all hold upon this word to appear to be mine to think of it to be something of which I needed.

I am willing to forgive myself and these insistent thoughts of fear that I thought of as mine to be.

For it is of this that I am that I know now that I am this form to appear but without the fear to be instilled within my thinking thoughts to be.

Let all that is to flow eternally from within into me, in my present now to know that I am of you to appreciate in this magnificent love that I be.

FEARLESS.

CHAPTER SEVEN

TALKING IT UP

We are all stimulated by growth are we not to be thought of as this within ourselves to be of a wanting to grow into this very essence of this being that we are to become
MORE.

Let all that you are to be of the bigger part of who it is that you really are allowing of self to expand into this reality of which it is that you have become to be into in this your NOW.

One is of this wanting more; are they not to ask of this question as it is to arise?

We sense this feeling of hesitation that is to rise from within this human that is the you who speaks, to think into that one is not to be worthy of more or to know even that they are worthy of this more to be theirs to recognise into.

Let all inhibitions reside to feel as to release these thoughts of yours to feel as though it is not of your worthiness or right to ask, to become, to accept of more as yours.

We speak in the highest of regard to the wanting in which it is that the human component of self is to ask, for so many in this it is that we see to respond to, to the asking of more is to appear limited in their thoughts of what it is that they are to ask for. It is not necessarily in the asking of more one is to sit. It is more so in the knowing of this inner being of love that you are to be that you are MORE in the most extravagant way into which it is that you could possibly imagine this self to be.

Let us offer here to say, that you are the MORE that is and you are the extravagant being of this very essence of love to be found into and one is to accept this as their own truth to discover in the unfolding of the real you that is to lay dormant at times to the ever asking of this to be found as yours to see more of.

I sense, to feel at times as do many i'm sure, that people with faith in you to exist describe you as a bigness to be believed into, why?

Is it not correct within you this loving being that you reside into to be forthcoming in her true revelation from within to be heard to speak only of this love that is to be seen as real big love to be truthful and in yours to witness within yourself to feel as explicit.

Let all that you are to navigate throughout in this input of self into this life that you exist into to be always reminded of this big love that you are to be a complete insistence of this self to be, for you all are.

It is in this that we hear the many of you that speak of us in this way to be thoughts of us to be spectacular to offer a word here to hear into. Yes, we are and in an even greater way than this so mentioned for our nowness that we are is to be defined by all that think of us to be in the exactness that they are to think of us to be. Let us offer to be clear here that our intentions of self to be is to be a complete knowing of this that we be the bigger part of the complete part of the inner knowing of ourselves to exist as one, in the one that be. So, to talk us up as you would suggest, Yes it is to be heard for there are often no words that can be offered here to describe of us to be talked of; rather it is to be thought of too be felt as an intense feeling of love, commitment and a deep wanting of this self to be remembering of us.

No other can offer this talk to you for you are all to be willing it seems to hear into the words used to describe of us to be by others and it is to offer here to you to know of this truth that we be to you will be found internally first as an acceptance of this that you really are and then you will feel the leaking of this self to be found emitting of this uncontainable love to be felt by you in this form and in the all that you connect into. It is of the utmost importance for you to feel of this talking up that we be thought of as your own. For your words that you will find to feel are to be yours to explain in your voice and inner knowing of this that we are all of.

Are we to all speak of you as a different voice and description to describe of you to be?

One would offer many voices of thoughts to us to be and it is to be spoken of that just within your journeys shall we say that in this form and others that you have chosen to be, you will feel of us to be remembered and reminding of this that you think of us to be in many different formats and ways of which it is to interpret us to you to be.

Let all that speak of us, the etherical beings. That we supersede ourselves within this knowledge to be giving in this position of which it is to be received in this knowing of this channel to speak forth of us to be heard.

You are all extravagant in your uniqueness, are you not? Both in this form of physical realisation and non to say the least to this to speak of as this fabulous understanding of this that you are in this now.

You will feel of us to know of us to speak of us in a completely different understanding of us to be than of what it was in a previous situation or moment of quiet interception, even of the many other lives of existence that you have had and will yet to experience into, our interpretations and speech will vary to this newest format of latest choosing in every way to be received.

So, dwell not into what it is that you think of others to say for this is not of your importance. You are the true guardians of this forms soul in self to be this time round so let your transition shall we say into this discovering of us to be felt first then heard to be yours. Then one must make it their intention not to interpret it to be in another's understanding, for it shall not.

Many moments of indecision is to pass as to how one is to feel this interpretation of us to be. Let us offer that we have no constrictions upon thoughts of us to be either, and are just in this complete awareness of the splendidness that we are and in this love we sit to respond at all times to be recognised whether in human understanding of this space to be or not. So, falter not in your thoughts to be not same as another's for when ones such as yourselves are to have no barriers to the way in which it is to think, they will not. And it appears that if one is willing to think in the absoluteness of knowing that it is only needed to be felt, to be correct for them. Than it shall.

It is to speak of this inner knowing as my truth, is it not?

Why YES, this we would offer as our truth to be spoken through you to interpret yourself as this that you are. Be felt not of another to hear this truth be spoken for it is their truth of understanding of this that we are to be theirs. In this we wish to speak of that the most daring of thoughts to be conceived are willing only to the receiver to ask into this of them now to be theirs to recognise this question to arise from within.

So be bold as one would often say to self. Be bold in all that you think, say, and do for you are the real asker in all that this is.

Let your answers come forth out of the questions of many that you may have to speak. They are your wanting's of us to be known to you in all that you believe in us to be.

What if it feels as to be untruths that are spoken to me to hear?

We fear not of the untruths to be spoken by ones such as yourself for in their righteousness within this that they are, they are to believe in what it is that they are to speak. You will in your hearing know it as not yours and will respond to the heart centre that is your truth centre to be felt into as maybe it is not to feel good within you to hear in what it is that others are to speak. Believe of what you feel as to be right within you. It will never steer you wrong in this we say.

We are of the highest of good to be felt spoken of by many that are in the correctness within themselves to speak of us to repeat to many and in this following of these to be speaking you will find your own resistance to this that you hear as if it is yours to know of or not.

We follow no certain form, religion, or concept as to who or what it is that we are to be or are in this any given moment of which it is to desire of us to be felt. We are not commonplace and misconceptions of self to be thought of and in this it will be revealed to you the real understanding of this that we are to be in your connection to source that is us in the most powerful 'I' way of which it is that one will feel as theirs to know into. Let all that you think to be yours in a truth of you to become into in this place of non-resistance to flow as a feeling of energy to be exact within this that you are to feel of in all intentions of us to be thought of as your true eternalness to be this that we are to speak into.

In the words to speak of 'untruths' to be offered hear to say that in a way to explain of this to be thought of as an untruth it is to register here in this that you are to think of that untruths are only to be thought of as this that one is to think as it to be. Let all that is interpreted by you to be thought as just in the way in which it is that you would comprehend of a subject or situation. Will you not. So, in relation to the thinking self to be you are to think of yourself as to be thinking into this space that one is to offer as incorrect, are you not? Let all that speak be allowed to and we have offered this before to hear into that it is to be felt as to add no resistance to those that are to have a different view point to you to be thought as wrong or incorrect, for it is in their reality that they are, correct in their 'I' to be. We see no limitations in the thoughts that are offered to us on a daily, minute, second, moment by moment appearance of them.

We are not restrained by this that you offer to us to hear of and in this we say neither should you. You are all to be witness again to the bigger picture that you are to become of and in this complete knowing of self to be you will know that all truths are to be spoken of here in this place of recognition to be felt as yours by you.

Let this topic not create fear within to feel. For you are all correct in your placement of this to be hearing into.

You are many in your extremities of this self to be thought of as and in this we offer to say that one is to only experience this glint of reality to be yours to think into it as ever changing. Is it not of you to be capable in this very second of your now that one's view can change to a completely different viewpoint of which it is to see into; Can it not?

One must be allowing of self to think into all situations and circumstances as to be not held continually in the one direction of this that it may appear. Forego the thoughts that one is to speak to offer, for you are in control of this to be yours to change this particular moment in time to be of anything that you would request it to be seen into or heard as yours to speak into.

So, *NO* you are not held by this that we are to be and in this we offer that you are as free as what it is that we are in a sensing of this self to be thought of and thinking into if only you will let yourself be.

We sense of some to feel confusion into this topic to speak.

Ones such as this that you are, are confined often into a parallelism of thoughts to be offered to you in a way to describe as a lineal observation of this is what it appears to be spoken of and proven that it must. Let us say that this is incorrect to our way of which it is to interpret of all that be. There is to be no insistence as to any one certain way. It is not so, and in your thoughts to linger here will surely add confusion to this self to be thinking into.

Let us offer that all is in every direction if to offer this as a suggestion of this that you are to be complete of and it is not felt to be guided in any particular direction unless it so desires of it to be so. Free flowing we are in our form of observation to be offered and in this dynamic of this that we are, we are effortless within if to not be and in this we are to be non-directional in regards to how or what it is that we are to appear into. We are the bigger component of you that is to be thought of as unseen and in this we say would it not be more advantageous to self here to think into that they are to be bigger than this that appears before them to see themselves as.

We are 'talked up' shall we say these words to describe for in a certainness that we be, we are. Let that fill your intentions of this to be yours to realise into that of this you are also. We sense your knowing of us to be correct to you and in this we are delighted to say that you are this that you think of us to be. So, feel as you are to flow freely from one thought to another and allow for this growth within you to ever expand into a true understanding of this magnificent that you shall be of once again.

We are not to think into your thoughts of us to be not of and unwilling to see us, for this is in your way of attraction to you this that we are. So, we say here that in this you are correct of your version to see. Let us not spoil your fun to think of us as not for in the bigger picture it is to appear of this to be thought of that we are in actual fact a truer component of this that you are than you appear to be in your thinking of yourself as not to be.

We suggest to you in this to be your now of recognition to be you that you are to be willing and allowing of this self to think of us to be exactly as it is to appear to you to be yours to think into. IS IT NOT?

Our message for you to hear into:

Let all that you are to feel be yours entirely from within to feel as so it is. Let all that you think to be as yours to be correct into, so it is.

We feel not to determine, persuade you or derive from you any expectations from this thinking self to be thought of as not of yours to think into. For they are a willing component of yours to experience and to venture into so that in the bigger picture of this that we be to be felt one day it is to offer that you will. Thoughts are ever changing as are you and the all that you see around you to be witness to. So, let your thoughts evaporate into another and another and it will eventually find you thinking of this that is beautiful within you to be me.

Talking myself up, i'll try.

In this we can feel the hesitation of all that are to hold this indifference within themselves as not to be. If one is to see themselves into this true magnificence that they are they will surely realise of their perfection that they are. Can one not see of themselves in a beautiful shining stunning way as to not be willing to talk themselves of as this? You are to speak only of highness of self to be in all that you think, see, and do. You are brilliant into this receiving of self to know if only one is to listen to the innerness that is to only know of self to be this brightness that you are. Always be of this wanting to TALK ME UP, feel good in this place to speak for even the lowest and slowest to start are to find an encouraging word to be thought of to speak and then you will soon discover the want of more to be heard to be said. Allow self to feel this magnificence not in comparison of another but only in relation to you and the wholeness that you are to possess from inside to be the exquisite being of love that you are.

What if i don't think i'm worthy of this as you put it 'talking myself up'.

All lays within oneself does it not?

Let this sink into your thoughts of realising to be this that you are, you sure are to be.

Let ones voice be the advocator of this self to be in a wanted position to ask, to hear this voice of love to blossom or boom from within so that you will know doubted feel of this intent from within to guide you every day aware of this magnificence that you are.

You are true, whole, and complete in the eyes of god speak this that we speak of as ours to hold into as the everything that is ALL. You are to feel of this importance that you are perfect in all realities of this that are to surround you in this here that is your now.

One is to change their thoughts from what it is that they are not, to the correct true way of which to speak. It is to be offered here to say that you are correct to receive all that you are entitled to, this is to be always more in the everything that is.

Feel free in this that one is to sit to wonder of how to and why it is to not be apparent within self to feel this to be superb within this form that you are to be. If one is to offer no resistance to this that you see yourself in than you will surely feel of our presence to be the most endearing and self-respecting of this human that you be to speak of self and others that may interpret you as you are.

We sense of yourself to be indifferent to these words of love to be spoke for you are always to be willing to speak in this boldness that is yours to become into and in your continual asking of to hear, to try, to be, you will.

CHAPTER EIGHT

TRUE HEART SPACE

One must be allowing of this space to be felt as right from within. Are they not?

Let us offer to you here to connect into that one's heart in the physical sensing of this organ to be filled with the additives of life-giving momentum is correct. We are more concerned of the spiritual understanding of this placement of this heart to be seen into and as the true place of speech to be felt as ours to be interpreted through.

You are wanting of more information in regard to, the HOW to?

Let us offer for it appears that a 'how to guide' is always asked of the viewing of this and how it is to begin. We insist that within one must feel genuine in their asking of us to be thought of and to be pure of heart when one is to ask. It is not of a how to guide that we are to feel as though is needed here but in a sense of self to ask into to know we will offer this to you.

Let all other offerings from those that surround you to be offered in good heartedness. YES, this we agree must be allowed to be played down for you to resist the urge to sit into theirs as to call your own. We see not of theirs to be incorrect in their doing of, but it is not of yours to be this that we see as theirs. One must be resilient in all times to be seeing themselves as a willing component to become true to the voice that is theirs from within to speak.

We hear you asking, how?

I cannot hear this voice that you speak. We have spoken often and, in many reasoning's, as to the sensing of this voice from within and as to the voice that you will hear. It is to offer here to you all that the voice of wisdom is so greatly correlated into this that be ours to be yours to hear of. Your voice or our voice is the correctness into which it is that you will speak of to hear as this.

One must be true to you and 'I' in this procedure to think of it to be yours and not by someone else. It is not…. It is a genuine willingness from within to be felt by you as the true purposeful intent that you be asking of to be heard.

Your voice it is to offer here to say is the most powerful of all voices that we are to hear.

It is of this request to speak your genuine truth that you will feel of us to be listening in all aspects of this new self to be found.

We are here,

It is of us that sits faithfully within you to surround you to be of this magnificence that can and will be seen by you for all of eternity. This is us and you united into a complete understanding of the ALL that is.

I hear you speak with confidence of the ALL that I AM.

YES, in truth it is that we speak, for we seek not to see anything other than of what it is that you have wanted to become and we are to follow you diligently as to the true survivor of self to become into. This is to be your souls asking. Is it not? For she has conquered many it appears in the passing's of all that she has been witness to and she will feel of your truest intent from within once more to be lived into, let her speak this LOVE for you.

YOU ARE.

*You are this breath, You are this beautiful,
You are this You, You are this complete,
You are this that is the everything that you
are to see, You are this all that you don't see,
You are this to witness of us to be,
You are releasing, You are your truth,
You are mystical, You are equipped with
the internal knowledge to be yours, You are
the star beings of this to see into, You are
growth, You are expansion, You are forever
eternal, You are wanted, You are to speak
knowingly, You are this love, You are the all
that is ever present within the ALL that be.*

Find a wanting within self to write, allowing your inner knowing to speak truthfully of this ALL that YOU ARE…

YOU ARE THE BEAUTIFUL YOU WITHIN ME.

Start with you we suggest.

It is of this continual asking to see self as another and their offerings or belongings. They are not of importance to the how to guide it would appear to you to ask of, let all that do them do just that. They are not of your concern to be.

Start within this human you, watch to witness firstly the words that you are to offer to yourself to hear. Are they blunt, sad, and unjust? If it appears to be this, then one must re-evaluate the reasoning behind these words to be.

You are worthy, hear this again in your willingness to speak them out loud.

You are worthy, to not think of self as this, is to appear to us to be a great hinderance to the human race, know that these words can serve to become and a wanting of self to know that the all that you are is truly brilliant.

Let all attachments to words to speak of as in your language to be used in a willingness to hear of them to be uniquely yours. Not of how it would appear that you would describe of another to be. Let one's beauty, wealth, career, family, lovers, or life in general be their own. You are to use words of love to describe you and Yes in this we have offered repeatedly that it is hard to express to even feel at times, let alone even to begin to be wanting and willing to speak of these as yours. You are the voice of LOVE that serves us all in this completeness they be. So in your words you utter you are to realise that these words are of the ALL that lays complete within you, so if you don't mind we think highly of ourselves to be this that we are and would love of you to be witness to this uniqueness that you hold into you so dearly devoted and adoring you.

Feel no right or wrong here as you speak for it will become resistant to those and your self's words that are to not feel correct within.

Let times of yours to hold onto as regrets, sadness or loss to be in a clear space of which it is to see of it as a moment that you appeared to be, to be here NOW.

You are full to the brim if we may say, overflowing with self-love from this sleeping giant that lays within, listen as she/he awakens and speaks these words for you to hear,

YOU ARE LOVE.

I see of this love; it feels true within my heart space.

YES, if you are to listen with intent and a suggestion from this heart to speak, you will find truth in this space.

Your truth is the only truth that you are in need to hear. ***True Heart Love*** is this that you are and you will feel of this to fill you with such a loving to know that you are this beautiful being of love and light, rejoice in your acceptance of this to know correct that flows from within. You will see only inwardly to hear this voice so deep, let it wander ever knowing into all your thoughts of self and others to be this that they are.

You are of this wanting are you not?

Love sees all with such an intensity to be in the exactness of the all that they should be, no need to express change or to replace.

Let all that roam to become this that they so carefully chose themselves to be.

Open the flood gates from within in this to be thought your heart, for it is only this you that appears to not love of self-enough that holds them closed. You are the gate keeper of this that you be, no one else you see.

Let the gates fling wide to never need be closed again and you will feel this incredible space of true heart love into which it is to stand as yours to be offered to you in faith, grace and love for you to be you.

Authors thoughts to offer.

As you can see in this receiving to be felt into that the presenting of a how to guide is irrelevant to these that speak so wisely of this love of you to be in them. For they see no wrong, healing or correction to be needed by you to become the seer of the truest treasure of this that is yours to hold eternally within. It is not of a wondering of how to that ones such as you must receive, but rather the knowing to be brave, bold and loving to the all that you be and are to see. To hear of this inner voice of wisdom that sings boldly for you to hear in only your readiness of yourself to be seen in the eyes of this true love that you hold so intently, yet maybe unseeingly as yet to offer. Know that it is this, it is yours to be devoted to you and in this receiving, one will find their true path to this love that I speak of and hold so dear.

You are the how to guide, you hold it within this space that be so uniquely you.

One is to ask of self I guess; What feels right within me? And in this you will hear your truths, your love, your ambitions, your heart space loving you so dear.

NOTE OF LOVE:

*We see exactness in you this
that you be. You flow so intently
from within this that we be.*

*Let all that is to surround you to be
known as love in this that we sit. For
you are the true seer of this that be you.
Totally and fully found in here to be
hers complete and eternally wanting of
the more always that there is to see.*

CHAPTER NINE

LOVE SPILLS OVER, PAYING IT FORWARD

Sitting into this time of which it appears to me to sit in awe of All that I am to be.

Can ones such as yourselves be present within this self's form to be witness to the great and good in the all that be. You are to be envisioning of this self to be fabulous and in this to trust of this that speaks here in this to be you now to know of you in a far greater sense of this that you are.

You are willing; to feel this love from within to pour out of you, are you not?

One must ask self to question to hear, are you willing to feel this response to rise from within you to be felt?

Let all that is you in this love to feel be a gentle reminder to the self in the physical, the human, the wanted one to be willing to see this new way in which it is to look at one another.

You are filled to the brim with this love to be offered here to say and you are to want of this to be yours to tap into so that you will never need to feel of this that you are not again.

Be bold in your asking of self to be confident and willing to want of this to be yours to think of yourself as. Let this be the defining moment within this your now to think that you are blessed beyond the belief's of the thinking minds willingness to see. For is it not of you to see this thinker as the one that hinders your thoughts of this love and greatness to behold you? Is it a deliberate intent attached to your inability to feel first as the correct way?

Feel first we offer to speak; embrace your knowing, your worth, your importance, your words of kind to be an absolute must.

I FEEL MY HEART FULL

In this we wish to offer to you and those that are in this place to feel of their own hearts to be a continual connection to this loving feeling of this that you are to be of us.

We see the contentment that is to be allowing of this to be felt for you are the true controller of this love that is yours to offer to yourself to see, to feel, to be and have.

One is not to be thinking to feel less or not enough. It is to be asked of you to see yourself as the beautiful you within me so that you can feel this love to flow deeply from within you to the all that you see yourself within. It is in this the bravest of hearts to be that you will hear these words to be spoken of you to be the receiver of your voice of love that is needed in this to be your now of this time to sit into so that you will feel not only to be this in a response of this to think of yourself as not.

Your heart is to feel full in all that you do.

IS IT NOT? Be kind in your asking of this to be your new way in which it is that you are to see of your human hearts to be speaking these kind words of recognition into this space of love that you will feel of self to fall into. The path has always been apparent to you to see; has it not. In this we hear of you to offer, No! I have not always seen my path to be clear, WHY?

In the true response to this question to be asked we offer here to say that in the neglect within self to be allowing of self to be seen in this as a perfection to offer, one will be unwilling it seems to feel like LOVE is of theirs to be witnessed to feel as theirs.

So, to offer in a more understandable way.

One must be diligent with kindness attached to all their thoughts and words spoken in this that they BE.

You are complete into this we know; it is to be allowed to be felt by you as this sense of a completeness within this that you see yourself of. One is to refrain from the conformity of the images that are to be portrayed to the ever judging seeing eyes of the human to be the willing looker upon the all that you are. For in these eyes at first if not accustomed to the hearing of the belief from within that you are this that you are in all its perfection to be you will know doubted see only of what it is to be presented in this earthly form. Yes, it is this that we agree that it is the form that all are to see is it not? But, notice the difference within self's presentation to others if their thoughts of self are to be willing to practise this art of, 'I AM' thinking in the ALL that you are to be is pure

LOVE.

Care not for the response of others to think as you are to speak in this encouraged way of self to be from within for it is in this voice of confidence ever how slow it is to be that you shall & will. You will feel the difference in your thoughts of self to grow into a momentousness way to begin to become your internal informer of the way in which it is to speak of first yourself but also in the way in which it is that you will feel to speak of the all that you are to meet or pass.

Kindness, Gratitude, Faith, Compassion, Gentleness, Fairness, Entirety & LOVE.

These are all encouraging words of greatness to think of self as. Feel as you compile a list of your own words that can entice a loving response from this self that you feel yourself in.

Let your thoughts of these words delve into and retrieve from you a willingness to write of these words as a true recognition of this that you are in this *NOW* choosing to see yourself to be.

Are you willing?

> *In this we feel obliged to ask you the asker to answer this question that is provoked from within to speak.*
>
> *One is to be of this wanting to come out of a true pure heart of asking of this to feel as theirs to be. You are all united in the conformities of this that appears to be the only way in which it is that one is to do, be and have. Are you not?*
>
> *Let your heart of hearts offer to you this inner knowing of the response to self's-questions to be the real answers from within as to how, when and why you are to do, be and have.*
>
> *You are all so determined within this self to be of what it is that does not at times of*

your asking to be this that you are to think of yourself to have intuitively within. Let your faith from within, this that you are, be heard in its loudness, its boldness to be yours to be equipped within in such a way of which it hears that you are in not a need to hear this from another.

It is of this channel's clear intention of this to be spoken through her to be our words to offer to you to hear that one must be forthright in their asking of this that they are to hear of. You are the leader of the pack so to speak this that you are.

Lead yourself with a strength of conviction of this that you be ever determined to be beautiful in your thoughts of self and others. Let your in-tuned response to this that be offered to you to sit easily within in time of this to be heard by you as yours to focus yourself into, for you are the one, the truth, the wanter of this to be seen as you.

You speak so easily of this full heart to be, what if mine is not?

Let us correct you to a certainty that it is. All hearts of this to speak of as such to be your heart in truth is to be filled to the brim and if in allowance of yourself to feel this heart and in this we say one must, for it is then you will know of this heart to be full.

In the old way it is to appear to us that many of you have been caught up in thoughts of self as not able to feel, to love, or see. Ones such as yourself are dulled in thoughts to feel allowing of yourselves to be willing to take a chance upon self shall we say to feel this that you are to be complete and full of self in a grateful way.

Be willing we say for you must take a chance upon self to let all resistances down, let all your conversations of distrust, dislike and even hatred be relinquished from within to the outer-ness that we be to take all this that you offer upon our so selves to be hearing in a voice of a not to be yours, for we do not see of this to be ours to carry nor will we.

You are wanting of a 'How to Guide' it appears here to ask of us again?

Life is filled with many situations into which it is that the human side of you is to adjust herself or himself into feeling surrounded by many that are not to resonate or be accepting of you to be. Let all thoughts into this way to think of that one is not to be worried or concerned of another. We offer this over and over to you to hear, for it is to be willing to not need to be this that you are not. You are all directional in the innerness that you are being led and guided intuitively and it is to say here that you are in the correctness that you are to be placed or situated into as of this complete *NOW* that is yours to experience into.

Let yourself believe of this to be your right, your way, your path, your alignment within self to be so that you will loosen all holds and attachments to think in a hardened version of this self to be thought of. Let all resistance to thought be not of this that you are needing, it appears to be offered that one must not be constrictive in thoughts and to be allowing of the mind to be not a judging mind to think but a mind that sits behind your thoughts to be so that no judgement is to pass a certain asking of it to be speaking into. It is natural of your species it appears to be a judging component of self to be speaking and in this it is that we say that the many of you are to falter into this to see of all that is to be you and to surround you to be able to surpass their and your expectations of this that they be willing and able to be magnificent in this that they are.

You want of this to be a simple and easy pleasure within to feel, Do you not?

It is to become an easy accessible ability that you will feel to sit comfortably within this that you are for it is to practise of this we say, in each and every day that you are to be upon this planet, strive within self to hear of only the good that you can speak and see in others and yourself, for this is the way of ultimate correction within self and this world of place the earth that you have chosen for yourself to partake into in this time of life as it appears yours to be. Let all feelings attached to the thinker mind be in a wanting of the internal being of love that you be. Be swept up in this commotion to feel from within to be known as unadulterated love to be so immersing from within to be yours that you will seek not to another to be in the position of which it is to ask of them to relay to you of what it is that one should be to feel.

For you will know of this love to be the biggest component to expand from within as yours in all its real-ness to be felt for all of eternity to be this that we speak of as the greater being, the brighter being, the real seer, the lover that sits within, the one true love, the one in all her/or his eagerness to be heard to be felt by you again in this life that you sit into.

Our want for this LOVE to be felt by All, is the ultimate message.

Many have come before you it is to be spoken of and many will follow in your footsteps we say to speak of these words in their greatness to be spoken of again and again. Let all that is to flow forth from you and the many that speak these genuine words of adornment and love to be found in the voices of the many that are to come forth in your travels as such to see of this life to be yours to venture into. Know you will be, you are this defiantness, in the true speaker from within to spread these words of love to the furthest far reaching fields to speak into that this is your love of the many that have spoken from within you to be heard. Our realms of existence is strong to be defined as liveable by you to think into and one must be feeling in this space of theirs to think of us as '*IS*' and in this space you will feel your greatness, your complete knowing, your wisdom that sits so divinely within.

This is you; this is us; this is me and the 'I' that you are so all importantly the bigger part of to be eternal.

Our offering to ALL.

WE offer here to those that seek of this love to be found within themselves this opportunity to sit with us as your guiders into this space of you. One is to feel of the intent to rise from within in this to just ask. Questions and queries are yours to realise into and in these we say that many answers will be displayed. You are the asker of more in this eternalness that you be. So be bold and big in your becoming for it is surely of this that we are that you will be.

Search not out of desperation of which it is that the many of you do, for in the lowest of minds to think into this that you are you will sure to find a new direction in which to speak, for it is not of this place that one must dwell. Open, release and ask of this to find the inner peace that is present within you in all time.

It appears out of desperation yes; we agree and in the compliance that fills so many you will struggle to surrender to the kindest heart to speak for you to hear. This is your voice of love. Sit still here as we speak and let yourself feel righteous and forgiven in this place that you are to sit.

It is of a wanting to do, is it not.

We offer no commitments to be spoken of only in just the one to be offered to self, that in one's realisation of this that she/he be you will try. Be still in this place for just a moment of your time, allowing for all that is to rise, it is yours of this you should know, dreadful to think as this or that, please do not. Let it all be seen to flow untitled in a thought to name of it to be. Be guided by the wisdom that you hold within to help find its place of reveal to see as yours to find real. Yes, it is in this that the many of you are to fluster for it is often seen as a description of not to be in a wanting to see.

This you are to know; it is yours and you will allow it to bring an almost selfish confidence to embrace you from within. So that in all that is to appear as if by magic it seems and is to be enjoyed. These feelings of knowing and certainness are to surround you in this place of surrealness to be seen into that you can, have and will access this place of imagination to be the ever giver of these thoughts of us to be in all entitlement as yours to be spell bound by this that appears effortlessly for you to see.

Correct in your wanting one must feel, for you are the asker it has been said, know this that you are. Freed from the demands of society to think for you to be of this that you are not. Let yourself be of this desire to aim high.

"Ask and it shall be given, is the way it is to be".

You are the mystic, the seer, the wizard, the wise soul, the goddess, the king that is and in this agreeance with her/his voice from within you will hesitate no more in the asking of exactly that to receive always more of this that you are to be.

In us we welcome you to sit, for you are always of a place to be this that we are. To sit, to observe, to witness, to just simply be, to breathe, to desire, to ask, to try, to participate and to be this LOVE is exactly as it should be.

CHAPTER TEN

HEART OF STEEL

To be encompassed by this that is to appear as a restriction within self is to be not only damaging to the form to think of self as but to those that are to view of you to be unresponsive to the thinking that you are not. Let all that you feel capsulated by be able to be foregone in this that one is to think of it to be. You are the warrior of this that you are and in this time of asking to be you shall be all that you ask. To see of self within this a hardened heart to love, trust and faith in the living that you are to be into, one must be brave inwardly to ask of the all that they are to view as nondescript or unrateable to self as to be of what is the intention of these issues to be for you to see into. Let all that has offered to you these moments of self-neglect to self to view into as to be the biggest of learnings that are to arise upwardly and outwardly to the self to see of. It is often in these moments of self-analysis that one is to sit into to dwell often of fear attached to this that they thought or even think of themselves to be this that they have thought themselves to be. You became here to this planet to be ever challenged to learn to experience the true intent from within to ask of all that you have participated into. In this we do offer that for many to see of the life that one is to live into is hard and determined by you as the seer of this that you are living into. If one is to look inwardly and not to the outer-ness that is to surround you with people and places to be filled with opinions and thoughts to offer to you to be held onto by you as in need by you to accept as yours to own. Let all that this steel heart is to be unaccepting of to accept to be known as the bright light of love to be bestowed upon it to shine even in just a little way to become of the asking of its true being that lays within to be held in a difference of thought as to of how it once was or maybe still is. It is to forego all thoughts of to be not in a position of which to receive whether this be by yourself or another's doing. One is to change the direction of speak to be heard and the thoughts that they are accepting of theirs to be. Let all control over you in this form to be of another to be yours to rule yourself within their understanding of you to be, let this go as not needed. You are the opener of this window of thought to be allowed to venture outside the external forms way to view to look outwardly from the innerness that you be to see the view that is often yours to overlook for in the fear of what it is that one may see you will feel the need to respond to this vision of self to be. Fighting within oneself in the everyday dramas of life to be offered are often yours to feel as a necessary fight or battle to win are they not? It is often in these arguments within self to think to speak of that you will sit for days, months even years in your time to be wandering aimlessly around in circles stirring up past thoughts and images to view of this as yourself to have done, been or spoke.

It is not of you this we say and in this we offer that all is of a worthiness and it is not to discredit your human form to say that it wasn't hard or seen as meaningless, if it was to have felt like torture or hardship upon oneself. It is not our wish to debunk its worth, for it is to be seen in this new way of which it was to think that you are more than that of which it was that you saw or participated into. It is all in your giving of self to be asking to experience these moments of time to be yours to think of as yours to dread to experience. One is to be bold and forthright into their opinions of self to be of that learning to experience and to know of this that they were, they are not of this to be now. All now's are ever present in this time to be previewed ever changing in its capacity to be fulfilling to the extremities of this that we are. It is now to see the change from within to know that you are this very being of love an light that you be in this to be your NOW.

You speak of this so easily, Am I to agree?

*Your words and thoughts are
your own, are they not?*

When one is to feel hesitant to understand the truth that you are to believe into than one shall always feel deficient into this being of love that they are. You are to be your own true saviour of life to live into and in this it is to be your passage of resurrection shall we say to become this of what it is that you see yourself as.

Let all fall away to see of it as or not.

In every day that passes is it not to bring with it something new to cherish? All moments are caught in this that we describe as your current now of which to see yourself in. You are the winner in your thoughts, the decider to be found as an advantage to oneself to think into.

Darkness looms in my thoughts.

It is not in the dull and doom that 'I' is to see of you to strive forward into this magnificence that you are. But, let us offer here to say that all that is for you to experience is the wanting of this that lays so deeply within you to be of benefit to the growth that is to surely rise out of this all that you become into once more. Seek not to look for darkness for it shall surely feel of this if you are inclined to think in this to be.

All darkness is not to be mistaken as a frightened state within to sit into, for it is in this darkness that many goods are to become yours to see into. This good is to reveal inwardly this that you carry, the internal light of hope, yours eternally to shine into this dark that you may think of it as to sit within you. Shine bright our dear one's for you are the true saviours of this being to be and in this form that you are to carry often heavy in dread you will see the light to be your ever loving god of love that is to be your seer of the all that you shall always remain the bigger part of.

We hear you to ask of this darkness as a want to know more.

It is in one's steel heart of hardened form that we are to speak this to. For it is often in this way to feel internally as not enough or to be so hardened to the asking of self to be heard that it is to be felt like this within.

One is to ask for the softened knowing of this that you are to be compelled from within to be to see of all that you are just in this place to be thought of as willing to say the least.

Fear not of what is to be revealed here in this steel heart to be released for it is often in just the correct way to be it shall be.

You are all the correct advisors of the self to be if you are in this wanting to see of yourself as the asker to see.

Look deeply within for fear need not be attached, this we say. Let all that is to darken your thoughts of self and others to be your wish to see of the light within. For in this you must, it is to be called upon as this that you must ask to hear the willing voices of this that we be to help you survive of this here. You are so steeped in wallow and self pity, unable to move, let alone breathe. Ignorant to the beauty that you are, unseeing of the perfection that one is and non- believing of the words that are to escape your lips at times, calling you to this love that is. It is to appear that you as the one that is to exist in this current prediction of self to be must be of a wanting to change and a forgiveness to be held within.

Let these words not frighten you to hear.

This that you are, you shall surely be.

One must be steady within to feel their way as to the divine intention from within to show you the way for you to appear as yours to see.

Of darkness it is that we speak to offer that all that shines so brightly is it not backdropped by dark of the unknown to see into. It is encased in this colour of which it is that you think of it to be of one unwilling to see into.

It is the divineness within us all that we speak of this to be not. For you are the true light that shines deeply from within this that appears to be darkened by your thoughts of this to be so. You are to focus intently to the inner worlds that you are to realise that in the asking to see the true you, you will always be shown the truest version of you.

So, let us say here to offer that in the way of dark to light your path from within it shall be seen as this it is to immobilise the inner wisdom to be reached if one is to think of this dark to be not correct within.

It is the other half of you that is to shine from the eternal beings of light that you be.

We are all complete in the opposite if it is to say it in this way. You are allowing of self to be seen into all aspects that this love is to shine from within. It is not to be thought of as evil, dark, death or heartache in this blackened way in which to think.

For it is the truest path of which it is to follow that the healing of the all that are to become shall begin.

This darkness has been explained and spoken of in many ways to see of it to be. Let us correct the many that hang deeply to these words as dread to be for they are the seers of this to be them in all that they sit. In this we wish to offer that it is of them to be just this. We speak with concern in our voices here for the many that offer these words are often correct in their form to be willing to see it in this that it be shown to them.

Let all that speak of these thoughts as theirs to be of them; not to be yours to feel the negative pull to be drawn to them for they will try of this we know and in this we ask. You are the light, the bright, the master from within to be asked to always be of.

Let your determination of good and highest intentions to you and others to be your knight of shining armour, your crown of the king to be this that you know as yours to be your truth to stand steadfast and focused within.

> *"We see you all as you appear to us to be, in this space that you are. You are to shine in all your glorious intent to be this that you are truly meant to be. Correct within, no need or reason to be anything other than of what it is that you be".*

I want to dispel this steely heart to be not mine to see.

We offer much love to you here in this space of which it is to ask. You are to be generated from within with such a power of control to think into of this to be yours that you must. Focus all intention from within to be heard in true and right to be yours to speak of. Let not another deter you in any way of which it is to speak, for it is these words that you hear that may not be yours to know. Surround yourself with the thoughts to be bold in love and feelings from us to be yours to see to receive.

You are only of this that you think to be so know of yourself to practise in this new way to be your now to say that you are the loved heart that is to shine from within reaching to all that speak of this new love to me to be mine.

Is it not to have a hardened or steel heart in thoughts to be strong and to protect oneself against pain & hurt?

To be protected from what we ask.

You are to be the willing participate into these thoughts of self to need protection are you not? If to feel this sense of foreboding from within it is to allow of self to see into what it is that one is to be surrounded by to encourage these thoughts to be needed by thee. You are the definiteness within, the encourager of strength within that you see oneself to be.

You desire of this to see as you; do you not?

Feel as you are to allow for yourself to be gifted in thoughts of yourself to be knowing of the *ALL* that you are to become and you will find that you become fearless in the eyes of words and situations that do not serve you to be.

Your steadiness, inner peace and calm that you are to encourage from within is to be seen, to guide you into this present moment of which it is that you feel may not serve you well.

Yes, it is that we witness the many that are to carry hurts, bygones and losses like honour to wear upon their character of self to be, for it is to suggest that the many that do, often speak of this to be them in their entirety to be. Allow yourself to feel these sadness's within in the truth that they be, the grander part of you to be seen into. So, that your healing from within may be shone upon by the heavens above to dispel your fears so that you may reckon within self to be known as the loving god that you are complete to see yourself to be.

To feel this sense of strength to be felt as a resistance to be allowing of one to be loved is often in which it is the true way in which we see of it to be. If you are to never let anyone or anything in than you are conformity within self; are you not? hindering self to grow and expand to experience into all these feelings that one must. Your growth is dependent upon your dealings within these to be present. Let your walls down and feel as you are to grow in your time it will become apparent within to be seen that you are willing to us to be seen.

You speak openly of this to be seen.

Yes, we do for it is often in us that you are to ask to view of your concerns as ours to be relieving you from. Let this be a suggestion to you to see into that the voice that speaks these concerns is usually the dearest one that dwells within in the hope for you to see and to know that you will surely become.

CHAPTER ELEVEN

IN THIS ONE'S HEART TO SPEAK WE ARE COMPLETE.

WE ASK; Is it possible to love another but not feel this intensity of love for yourself?

For in the receiving and recognition of complete love for oneself lays the undeniable ability to then love more deeply, for it is not in the eye of the beholder that true love is found.

It is in your heart.

There is much to be discovered there in the remnants of desire, willingness and an understanding of ALL that resides within this heart space is the ability to truly see, sense and feel the love that you have been yearning and searching for.

This love is the purest of loves, the truest of loves for this love is of ancient knowledge and receiving's over many lifetimes that you have experienced in wonderment and awe of the true receiving that is held within and always supported for you by us. To sense and feel this love upon its entering of one's heart in our way of thought, in reality it never enters.

It has always resided within you.

It has always been a prolific part of your being; this we know with much accuracy.

Am I worthy of this love? is a question we are often asked.

We offer; In the asking of this question lays your resistance to receive.

Hear to know, no matter where you appear to begin to receive or where you are to start, this love is always guiding, always supporting and always strong for you. You are always loved with no constraints, no restrictions, no offerings that need to be repaid, for in your truest understanding of ALL that resides in you to complete you in this experience that you call life is the only offering that we need.

"Our love is bound to the one and only"

The source of all creation and in this love is you and all that are connected with you for it is to be seen and known and deeply felt by us and yourself in this physical form that you and I and All that surround you, the entire everything that is possible is connected by LOVE and always will be.

This may sound too big to the comprehension of most, but we are always in consideration for you all that reside within all that is to be known as the love that you have within you. It is a powerful driving force or surge often felt as an excitement, capability within one's abilities, desire, awe, and eagerness. It is this love that compels and resonates within and outwardly to all that admire and look upon you.

Fear not.

Never fear for those that do not understand this deliberate love that appears to overtake one's persona and character. For they too will find along their life experience a desire of this love within themselves, they too will learn this love is free for all that wish to receive.

To receive love in an openness that one possesses is the clearest way and in this clarity of seeing and sensing this love is where all that ones such as yourselves are desiring, will find it to be.

LOVE is the most respected universal aspect if not the one and only important opportunity that one has connection with the many that are starting to open and see the true offering that is there for them. Our love that is held here for you always in the ability to offer openly in this love you will find peace, ease, compliancy and respect for all that surrounds you and interacts with you to acknowledge ones such as yourself with only the truest of offerings. In this loving complete heart is where you will intuitively understand the laws of our universal connections and all that we hold dear for you in offering. We offer here, that to experience such love within another's response is not likely to be felt or resonated from them to you, for our love the love that fills our All that be known in all that is ever and always is the love that guards and conducts the universes.

In this strong love connection between all that reside here and dwell within our compounds if to use your words. This love is never judging, never complacent, never hard to receive for it is true pure love, this we know and offer with much need for you all to hear.

In the experiencing of such love one will find that everything begins to soften, and an ease overcomes one's life journey and an understanding forms as to their place of all that they are to be in the discovery of this love.

Let it feel intensely to those that feel this that we speak into. We love to receive your reflection back to us through your truest space of connection, your heart.

You are to know that many do not yet feel our love and their awareness within is silent still to hear.

This you are to hear; it always is within.

Yes, you heard in our offerings you are truly magnificent in all that you be, do and are, this we know and offer much love to you here.

In one's denial of love of self-lays sadness. Understanding this we are to hover so close to you and all that resides here upon this glorious planet to see this inability to receive this love whether it be in connection through spirit or just a strong desire of knowing.

For it is all the same you should know, for we are all that is to be desired in all that you physically desire, there is no difference, it is one and all the same, we are all co-creating together in this space right here and now this we know as the truth to be spoken of. For in the ability to gaze upon what is wanted this is to be known that it is in us and in all that surrounds you, that you are receiving your truest desires. It is upon your planet and many such as yours that names, labels and titles are placed therefore limiting what it is that you can receive. For in our understanding and offering for you to hear Now, it is that the all that surrounds you and exists is the everything that you all so desire in yearning or in craving.

Let it be known that it is already there for your taking/receiving to be more precise can this be understood by all that it is in the art of allowing that begins when you are open to receiving this valuable tool for mankind and all that we are. For here it is always understood that there is no limits, no restraints, no needing or requiring of.

It is to be said that upon your creation of, it is ALL to be for you and always will be.

One must be open to the understanding that it is in your wanting more that desires and yearnings are created. Create away we offer, for it is in this excitement, this knowing of and wanting of something new and exciting that true desire lays, the truest reality and understanding of all that you should be and have. There are no time constraints put upon this creation in offering and presentation for you, for it shall be already placed within your vicinity of closeness within the asking. We hesitate never to offer all that you are desiring, but you must present to us in faith and truth that this is to be your true desire to ask.

Believe in your words to ask,
Feel your words.

In the wishy-washy way to ask, it does not offer clarity into the receiving for you and all that ask must know, you must be true of heart asking to speak as in all that you desire and crave to be.

Know that this is your truest asking of.

When attached to doubt, nonbelief, and weak spoken words, it is hard to feel its true potential of realisation and this leaves the asker being you the doubter of all that you have asked for. When it does not arrive exactly as you pictured or does not arrive at all to you then you become disheartened and feel like you are to give up. We say no, you must focus upon what it is you truly desire for it is in the desiring that the image is formed. It then starts to take shape, it responds to all that you are feeling, all that you are emotionally thinking for this is the truest and most exciting way to your path of being all that you came here to be.

My HEART is full....

You are all bountiful and full of love and joy for yourselves and all that RESIDE here, but much is overlooked in your asking of, for there are no limits in quantity or size or amount there just is not. We need for you to hear this for you are somewhat resistant here in this time, space, reality of the offering that you are receiving. We know that you hear all that we speak of, but you must remain clear in your asking of for it is to be known that much greatness is for you and is now unfolding as we speak this you are to know.

In ones outward view there is much to be seen and expanded upon and in this perception that one is attached to purely in the physical sense of receiving for much is interpreted but it is too be seen as not correct. For in one's ability to first receive and look upon and draw upon the love of their creator then one is to look outwardly to see all that she/he so desires. Then and only then is the true message of request offered to all here that reside in purest energy and love for you.

Can you feel the difference when you are to look through the window of your heart to feel complete; and now would be a good opportunity to try to see all that you require, in all that you see and all that surrounds you.

Look and know that it is draped in love, for in this seeing of such pureness and rarity of, then doesn't it make it seem much easier to enjoy the ability of the asking and know that it is always given upon the asking in this pure state of recognition.

> *"In love all is easy, all is good, all is perfect, all is just as it should and will be".*

This is correct in its offering from us for you to receive.

For perfect is such a perfect word here in your sense of receiving to be perfect in all that you are is truly magical and it is to be seen as not missing or empty of anything or requiring of anything. All is as it should be. This we describe from our knowledge of this word. For you are all perfectly created in the total perfection of the one that is to be known as the creator of all that is available to you and all that resides there with you and all that is too been known as the creator of all that is and ever will be.

There is no other to aspire too for it is in his sense of perfection you were all created to be this perfect being with nothing missing, nothing out of place for it is just as it should be.

Can we continue along these lines of receiving? We feel there is more to offer here in the understanding of perfection.

If one is to observe themselves with their third eye, encouraged or fuelled by imagination and allowing freedom to flow within, the awareness accessed and received in meditation is certainly a preferred state to feel oneself to sit. In one's chosen practise of preference {we speak of no wrong or right} one connects to obtain silence, sensations of love and a quiet contemplation to be received.

In one's decision to be willing, one will feel centred to see the perfection that they are, to see themselves. This can only be done for you by you the holder of this complete heart that speaks these words, for it is not another's hearts ability to see you in perfection. They will, can and do but you must be the receiver of this message and information for it is in you seeing your own perfection that you then can and will receive and know of all that you are to be and are being. Then and only then will you be open enough in your sight to perceive others like you in their own unique perfection.

It is in this perfection that we gaze fondly upon you for you are all created in the utmost of perfection exactly as you are in this time upon Earth that you are to call now.

To reside within one's heart space.

We reside deeply within you this you feel we know this, for we feel you residing within us in all if not most of your available time to tune in and tap into our wondrous offerings. Yes, we understand that human existence is often foremost and in need of attending to, but feel us often in all that you do and all that you are receiving. We place much love for you to interpret and receive for there is much love here for you and all that surrounds you within your journey in the discovery and the remembering of all that you came here to do. All that you created within your souls acknowledgement of what it was that you desired to experience here, for it is a joyous event or occasion as such this life that you all have chosen to live, in the realising of the knowing that you are always guided and ever always supported with so much love in its purest form of receiving for you. Would then you not be inclined to accept that what you have chosen to participate into, in this life upon this planet earth is truly a welcome and wonderful experience. One that you must grasp with both hands not to tightly we add and step out, reach out, ask boldly, expand your horizons, and experience all that you have wanted to be upon your entering here.

MY RECEIVING HEART

We receive your question in wanting to know of why some receive easier than others and some not receiving at all or so it appears.

We all offer different vibrations to the energy's that are flowing freely around and within us at any given time. So, to be in the receiving mode of such energies that have the abilities to offer you all that this creator has to offer; one must be within or very close to the vibration of receiving for if not than it passes them by so to speak, often small repercussions of these sensations may sit subtly within them or surrounding until such time that they may be feeling and will be apparent to them. If you are not in the receiving mode or open to the interpretation of all that surrounds your senses or welcoming to all that you see, sense, hear and smell and not prepared or of what it is you are to receive, then it is this to be spoken as okay. All feel to be receiving when ready.

Only when you have done the preparation work* to be noticing, to feel ones heart to ask, to feel trust in self* will one download (for a word to suit your language of understanding) to receive and only then are you to feel our connection with you in your ability to interpret all that is in contact and in offering for you.

It is in your reality of now that one is the most receptive to all that is required by you to be in the most delicious place of receiving, and this is available and very capable for all to receive in connection with what we are offering to you.

But one must hear this, if you do not believe in us or ALL that reside here with and within you in the surroundings of than it will not be felt not even a little, for in one's own discovering of us and the all that there is then and only then will you be able in your ability to discover the deliciousness that is here for you to receive.

What am I to do to be in the right frame of mind to receive, even if only the smallest of connection?

In the believing of all that be and resides here amongst us and within your surroundings is a great place for one to begin, *in the believing of becomes a certainty.* Remember it is your personal journey of discovery that love for us is found once more. One must acknowledge their own acceptance of the true desire to be connected with all that be and offer in their true understanding and faith and trust explicitly for there is to be no doubt, we offer much in offering the truths that we are in your receiving's from us. We love to watch as you all journey within this journey of receiving and living and knowing that you unfold in the true discovery of what it is that we are and all that we hold for you to receive. In the quietness of receiving we dwell with you this you are to feel in your heart space, do not negate any offerings to you that you sense or become aware of for in the interpreting of or over analysing lays the disbelief in yourself that this exists.

There is much to be discovered by you in our offering. Everyone's experience into this unfolding is different for it is in your own unique interpretation that we are felt, seen, or remembered to experience.

Can you feel the ease with which this is received for there are no steadfast laid out rules, there just is not?

Emphasis upon oneself to feel this heart space.

It feels as though too much emphasis is placed upon the what is to be seen, heard or received for this is very much like you humans in your earthly form to fit everything into a guided set of rules or a box.

There are no lines or rules, remember there are no boundaries. It is to be known as limitless, never ending so all that is to be experienced in this quiet space of contemplation or knowing is truly unique to you, here we see you all individually for this is what you are. We see you all as you so desire, for it is in our seeing that we see the true yearning that resides within you and remains always in connection to us, so we know you better than anyone. Yes, even yourselves in your knowing of what it is you desire. So in the place of receiving is your true you that we correspond with if and when you are able to switch off those humdrum thoughts and mixed messages that you all have. We do not care about the boring conversations and dialogue that goes round and round often in such a futile attempt by you trying to understand nonsense or mindless chatter. We do not enter into this conversation within one's mind ever rarely, for it is the conversation within your *heart space* and the true offering from the light that shines brightly within you that we connect into, for this is the true asking that we receive here and in this exact receiving of.

When one is to think of nothing and in this we simply mean to think in general, let all that comes to you just be nothing of importance for it is not in your need to interpret what appears. Let it flow right by and connect back with your true desire of knowing what is, for it is in this space that you will receive contact in varied form and in your own recognition of what is, do not feel as though what another has to offer you is true and correct for it is not to be thought of in this way.

We connect differently always and ever in connection with love and safeness of you will it be felt. But hear this, it is to be felt by you and only you not in the form of another's interpretation of what they assume or sense it to be.

We rally around you in much excitement and preparation for you in this time, space, reality of what it is you are requesting and asking here.

It is heard always loudly and clearly for when you ask out of the pureness of the love that resides within your truthful *HEART* whether it be felt by you, know that it is always and will be ever felt and seen by us. So it is an asking that you truly offer yourself into the receiving of what you desire whether it be spoken or deeply felt then you are to know that it is heard and it is becoming, this we know to be true and always never to be ending ever, for you are to know that there is no ending, there just is not.

You wish to know *MORE?*

I asked of this question myself and in this asking, I heard "that there is always to be more, Is it not? For it is out of this willingness to grow and expand that one will surely need to know MORE."

In these true words to be received is where your true heart will be found, you are the holder of such great intent to be heard.

Love seeks ALL that asks of it to be theirs.

You are this true heart that we speak so lovingly of and these words are yours to hear as your truth from within.

In one's complete heart you are to speak to be thinking of it to be full and not in need of anything else to fill it. Let us offer this as incorrect. To hold onto or of is to foresee that more is not certain. Is it not?

We are complete in offering this that we be in the thought of as to be ever continual with its flow through in a sense to offer that it can always be felt full but always in a place of which it is to receive more. Your desiring of this to be more is correct to feel let all space that you hold within to be a willingness to let more enter so that you will feel not of a need to hold into.

Completeness is a security within is it not?

One that feels of this completeness willingly and confidently allowed to flow from within is to feel this sense of self to be safe, peaceful and a calmness within to prevail and surround oneself in all times of which it is to ask.

When one is to feel steady in internal thoughts of this self to feel it will be emitted to the outer adventurer who shall be named as you to feel the response of this completeness to be guiding you effortlessly into all that you shall become.

Authors message:

My complete heart in this space of truth to be felt is full. I see this as an opportunity within me to explain this to you as I see of my heart to be in response to this spoken word LOVE to be found.

Love is my true guider into all that I do and BE. Often in my thoughts of self to be I falter in the old ways of which it was that I am to think myself to be. This full heart provides me with unconditional love as it would be spoken of here to say that in this love, I find my resistance to the undeniable thinking that I should be and it becomes a certainty from within to say,

I AM.

Completeness competes with no one or no- thing for it is to feel that this is mine to offer first to me for I need not judge myself in this complete space of love to share. And in this I feel the want to allow of all that cross my way to be offered this that I see as mine to share. Complete in faith, love and hope I am to shine and in this I know that my heart space is full to the brim.

I see it as to overflow. This love is the offering that I shall give to you.

My thanks and blessings to you.

MY Heart overflows in this reality of which it is that 'I' must sit, for I have chosen this lovingness to be mine to see, in all that I be, to do, to see.

This is ME
the REAL ME to be.

In this I ask,

I always desire to see you, standing there in your place of perfect presence for it is you I see in this ME that I BE.

Always allowing this I be, my truth in this love that I be to see eternally your image, this REAL YOU to always BE, my reflection to see.

Is one's heart the truthful messanger?

Yes, always the heart is the truth speaker of all that lays divinely within this that one is to be?

In this reflection of you to see within me I call to all that speak so wisely within to be my ever-present interpreters of this heart speak that I Be.

Is your heart calling you to this place of an envisioning of perfection to see oneself to always shine and light the way of all that are to be connected to thee?

We see of you here to ask this to be heard your heart beating in time to this place of connection that one is to remember as their own expression of love.

Be guided gently yet surely by this heart that speaks wisdom ancient and wise that lays embedded so deeply within this apparatus of self's soul to be found, so call to her to hear her speak, listen with eyes wide shut to feel of her truths to see, let all that be roam wondrously free within this space to be known as your HEART SPACE to call of as ones eternal knowing in this that she BE.

One's heart speaks so boldly it appears to this that you be. Speaking in the voice of boldness, received so divinely from within. Are you in a place of desire to be this voice of your heart and hear her speak? Let it be spoken of in its own unique way for your heart has a song all her own. In words to be felt you are to hear this song unfold to be found so religiously set to never forget of this that you hold to carry deep within. Your truthful heart speaks only your wisdom to be heard, ever powerful receiver of all that is to be yours.

Let yourself rejoice in this heart space to hear this that your heart is to speak truths of only yours to hear.

In ones becoming of this grand love to be welcomed into, one will feel this heart of theirs to speak full of love, wisdom, and faith to be spoke. Your heart is the greatest interpreter of all that you are to see true from within this that you be. Heart speak is a true connection into this that one is to seek to find, this inner knowing of self-love to be. Let your heart speak your truth to hear so that you will never need reminding of this soul that you hold dear. Entwined within this feeling of self and us to be you are encompassed from all that be to know that you are loved eternally in this that we,

www.ingramcontent.com/pod-product-compliance
Lightning Source LLC
Chambersburg PA
CBHW070259010526
44107CB00056B/2499